The Box I Live In

Corey Harper

ISBN: 978-0-578-97769-0

Limits of Liability and Disclaimer of Warranty

The author and publisher shall not be liable for your misuse of this material. This book is a non-fictional work and created strictly for informational and educational purposes.

Warning – Disclaimer

The purpose of this book is to educate and entertain. The author and/or publisher shall have neither liability nor responsibility to anyone concerning any loss or damage caused, or alleged to be caused, directly or indirectly by the information contained in this book.

Book Design by Anna Mikhaela

Table of Contents

Dedication

To our warrior,

You fought your battle, and we know it was a hard one. We love and miss you more than you'll ever know. Everyday isn't easy, but we're all doing the best we can. Rest now, king. We'll take it from here.

Introduction

Waking up today, I thought it would be like any other day. Working from home throughout this pandemic has led me into a pretty standard routine: wake up 15 minutes before it's time for me to clock in, walk my dog, wash my face, and brush my teeth before finally opening my laptop and starting my shift as an online mental health coach. Sometimes I manage to squeeze in a quick breakfast before being inundated with non-stop clients seeking mental health services and Zoom meetings, which I could sometimes do without. But I enjoy helping people, so it's typically worth it. And yet today, I never could have imagined what this day would bring. I guess that's the irony of life; you never know what it will throw your way. In an instant, you can see all of your dreams come to life or witness nightmares uninterrupted.

As I pushed through the seemingly innumerable number of clients, I received a call over Facetime. Of course, the Wi-Fi connection was shitty, so I struggled to hear what was being said and because of the mask they were wearing *(because, you know- COVID)*, I couldn't tell if they were laughing or crying: it was the latter. What I heard next will likely reverberate in my brain for the rest of my life: *"He's dead. He killed himself."* I was stunned to my core. It felt like a punch to the gut and I was speechless because of the life that we would never get to see through. In an instant, I thought of the children I would never see him father, the wife I would never see him marry and the fruitful career he had ahead of him. I guess, while my initial reaction was that of complete disbelief, I also couldn't help but think of the last time I saw him.

We spent Christmas Eve together, and amidst everything going on with the pandemic, it was a blessing to have been able to gather at all. It wasn't lost on me how special that moment was, but I never could've guessed how precious of a moment it would be to me and the rest of the family. For gifts, he handed out gift cards like they were candy, with his brother especially basking in the Starbucks gift card he was given. It's funny how vivid memories can become after a tragedy. I can still picture it like it was yesterday: him running down the stairs, dressed in a t-shirt and basketball shorts, warmly embracing everyone that walked through the door, myself included.

In fact, now that I think about it, he was boasting a bit that day because he had helped his parents prepare dinner for everyone. I gave him his props and was sure to pack my to-go plate well before it was time for me to leave. But mostly, I remembered his one-of-a-kind type of humor. I remembered his laugh and the way he could tell a story like none other. It was his larger-than-life personality and nuanced views of the world that always had me captivated. I chose to reflect on who he was for most of his life, not who he was in his final moments. His final moments could not possibly sum up the totality of who he was and how he lived. He was so much more than that final and fatal mistake.

As I drove to be with my loved ones, I kept thinking about the transference of trauma that had occurred today. The trauma and struggles within the deceased did not dissipate with him; it only transferred to those who had the unfortunate task of discovering his remains. That image will stay with them for the rest of their lives and that breaks my heart. The death in and of itself was devastating but knowing that those I love will always have to live with that pain completely shattered me. I cried for the life lost, but also for the pain I could not save them from. I think somewhere inside me, I wished I could take away their pain, their trauma. Some part of me wished I could have saved them from that visual. Like if God allowed me to extract that one pain-stained memory from their head and put it in my own, I would have.

The reality of arriving at the home, where the yellow "caution" tape had just been taken down from around the perimeter, was arriving to see a grief-stricken mother, unable to reconcile the violent end to her child's life. The sound of her cries will live with me forever. In her voice, I heard the years of parenting and love she bestowed into her child, the years of working her ass off to give him everything he could ever want or need. In the tears of his siblings, I saw the future of a brotherhood, the plans of growing old and raising families together that will never come to pass. In the eyes of his father, I saw a man visibly shaken, knowing that he'll never see his son walk down the steps again and greet him like only he knew how. It was almost like an outer-body experience.

The blood-stained carpet and clothing in the room were like a scene I had once seen in a movie, but nothing I ever thought I'd see with my own eyes. You never think you'll see something like that or that anyone close to you would ever experience it. I quickly turned my gaze from the spot where his life ended to the rest of the room: where he lived. Walking through his room, I saw remnants of the shadows he'd left behind. There was so much we didn't know, so much we still don't know. Like many of us, he kept his shadows in the dark. I think so many of us wake up every day, thinking that we have an infinite number of moments left with each other, moments to laugh, moments to cry, and moments to feel. But we don't. Our moments are indeed finite, they all come to an end, and they are never promised. The entire experience of it all was like a weird nightmare that I know we all desperately wanted to wake up from. This was a stark contrast to how I thought my Tuesday would go. It was inconceivable to me that by the end of the day, someone I know and love would be dead, but that is the reality of mental health and the struggle to manage it.

While there are many suffering from varying mental illnesses across the world that will not meet the same fate, there are many who are contemplating it. Within the black community, there is so much work that has to be done in reference to mental health awareness, destigmatizing mental health and creating more effective and accessible mental health services. I don't know if even all of this could've prevented his death, but maybe it could've helped. Who knows, right? But his story is a reminder of why I decided to write this book at all.

We've all either gone through some shit, are going through some shit, or will go through some shit at some point. My own philosophy is that we are all always, at every stage in our lives, going through something, but talking about it and getting help for it is what matters. In the society we live in, especially in the era of social media, everyone is striving for perfection or at least the appearance of it: it's truly maddening. Imagine how many lives we could save if we were all transparent and honest about those skeletons in our closets or the parts of us that we'd rather not show the world; like those parts of us that society tells us aren't beautiful or social media worthy. I'd like to remind you that you are wonderful the way you are, and you are not alone- *ever!* You are so much more than whatever battle you're fighting, and I can prove it.

When I set out to begin crafting this project, I wanted to pull together individuals who may have experiences that you can relate to. Black women and men who have experienced their own fair share of mental illness, came forward and told me that they wanted to tell their stories. I sat. I listened. I wrote. Their names have been changed in order to protect their identities and other individuals discussed in the book. Also, below their names, you will also find their preferred gender pronouns.

Throughout the book, you'll also find some helpful information that sheds light on the severity of mental illness within the black community, information that you may not have previously known. Through their stories, I hope you find comfort. I hope you find community and maybe even similarities. I hope you find hope. But most of all, I hope you find yourself, seeing yourself represented in their stories and knowing that life always awaits on the other side of the pain you're going through. In their own words, these are their stories.

Trouble in Switzerland

Olivia's Story

She/Her

Growing up in Shelby, North Carolina was a bit of a sobering experience sometimes. Living in a place with only one county and four high schools was a bit different than the seemingly larger than life essence of Atlanta, which is where I've been for the past few years. I grew up near pig farms, picking pears off trees as a kid, and rolling down hills barefoot: to say my hometown is different from Atlanta would be an understatement. Shelby is about an hour outside of Asheville and about an hour away from Charlotte. Because it's so small, I'm never surprised that most people have never heard about it. The city is literally like one of those places you see in the movies: the town shuts down for football games, there's nothing but Walmarts and yes, everyone is my cousin somehow. *(No seriously, when I would meet people and find out their names, my first instinct became running back to my mom to see if we were related to them or not).* In fact, my graduating high school class only had around 180 students in it. Everybody knows everybody. But for the first 18 years of my life, Shelby was home, even when it didn't always feel that way.

My grandmother, the woman I call mom, adopted me after I was born and raised me. For reasons that are still a mystery to me, my biological mother gave me up, which was probably for the best. To say my family dynamic was a bit hectic, would be putting it mildly. While my biological mom gave me up for adoption and allowed my grandmother to raise me, she raised my younger sister. My biological dad has 14 kids. *Yep, you read that right.* As the story is told, I am what they called, "The First Non-Bastard Kid" in the family, as in my biological mom is the first woman that he married and had a kid with. I have two older siblings that I don't know well, and I guess you could say that I was the acknowledged grandchild, *(and of course my siblings didn't take too kindly to that phrasing).* My dad cheated on my biological mom with a woman he would go on to have three more kids with and after that...I only know from my other siblings that we have other siblings because the age difference is too great. I believe my oldest sibling, my brother, is 34 years old and my youngest sibling is maybe nine or ten years old...*I think?*

While it was crazy growing up in that kind of dynamic, I didn't know my upbringing wasn't normal. I guess, in my world, in that town, everyone's lives were that chaotic. Everyone had multiple pieces playing at the same time. You know, a lot of people had dads who had multiple kids all over the place and had grandmothers raising the kids and neighborhood kids being raised by everyone we call "Auntie." It wasn't until I got to therapy in college where my therapist was like, "Well, you know, that's not how things are supposed to be." My response was, "What?! You mean to tell me that a lot of people don't live like that?! News to me!" *Shooketh!* It was all completely normal to me. Growing up, knowing that my biological mom lived in the same town, raising my younger sister, was a bit surreal, though I didn't learn that she was my biological mom until I was around seven or eight years old. But once I found out and anytime she'd come around, I was sure to let my mom know that I didn't want to go home with my biological mom. Why? *Because I didn't like her*. It's that simple.

However, I still keep in contact with my biological mom since my mom is getting older and my sister has kids. I'm only connected to my biological mom because of my mom. I haven't seen my dad since I was 13 years old, and I'd prefer to keep it that way. He only kept in touch with the boys, for some odd reason. I found out that my brothers have been in contact with him the entire time, but my sister and I haven't seen him in years. If I were to ever ask him why that is, I feel like I would be lied to the entire time. He's a compulsive liar and he'd make excuses for everything so I'm more than at peace with keeping my distance and living my life without him in it. Looking back, I can see how I found solace in everything outside of my family in order to get through those times.

I mean, I guess survival instinct kicked in and I said, "Fuck it!" I think it used to hurt when I was young, but by the time I was 10 or 11 years old, I told myself that I have to do what I have to do in order to never speak to them again. I was like, "Oh, so how great do my grades have to be for college? How many sports do I have to participate in? How many things do I have to be involved in to not go home? And when I am home, how many video games can I play, or books can I read to not be completely present with the family? And then, what can I do in order to get away from this town?" None of this is meant to paint a negative portrait of my life at home with my mom and step-dad because, for all intent and purposes, my actual home life was good for the most part. I simply found that living in the family system I was born into was a bit chaotic and I didn't want to be a part of any of it. I didn't want to be a part of the drama, dealing with my biological parents and siblings. It was stressful and a bit daunting existing in that kind of chaos when I so desperately wanted peace. Eventually, I found solace in doing my own thing and forging my own path. But even dealing with all of this, I can say that I'm blessed to have the mom that I have.

My mom was a preacher, which was always a troublesome thing because she's a once divorced woman who preaches and in these country places, they don't tolerate divorce. It's one thing to be a woman in the pulpit, but a divorced woman in the pulpit? *Sexism strikes again!* Also, of course, like any kid, I wanted to do what my mom *(who I adored)* did, but by 10 years old, I knew quickly that I was not going to be religious. I think a lot happened at that age. My mom had gotten married to my step-dad and we had to move churches, moving from a church where everyone knew me to a church where women weren't allowed to wear pants. I remember asking the pastor, "I get how Jesus was born but how was God born? Because you talk about God like He's a person." And he never answered my question. He continued stating how God created Heaven and Earth, but he never answered my question, which meant that someone was lying, and I didn't believe a soul after that.

But of course, I still had to do Vacation Bible School, second services, Sunday school, choir rehearsal- the whole shebang, but I got as far away from church as I could once I went to college. I kept trying to attend church my freshman year of college, out of habit, but it didn't feel good to me. I started questioning if I ever actually identified as a Christian or was I only doing it because my mother was a Christian? *The answer was yes*. But it was hard talking about it with her because, to her, God and the church saved her life, but for me, it was the opposite: it was suffocating. As opposed to feeling like there was someone guiding me, I felt like I was making the decisions in my life, not some presence in the universe making my decisions for me. Of course, my mom thought I was an atheist, but I didn't. To be honest, I don't know what's out there, but I've always had an interesting relationship with the idea of religion and God. It's not that those things need to be proven, I simply don't understand the cult mentality behind not questioning things. I was questioning everything!

My mom and I don't quite see eye-to-eye on that, but I respect what religion has done for her in her life. She loves God like she loves being a mom. She feels like her role in life is to be a mom and I think it shows. I was blessed to have a parent who loved me, kept a roof over my head, and reminded me every day that I was loved, which by looking at my biological parents, I could've had the opposite. If there's any kind of downside, then it is that she was very enabling of herself and others growing up. It was obvious that she was doing her best, but she kept behaviors she shouldn't have. For example, if you were to tell her, "You hurt me by doing...", then she would immediately respond by making it all about her and what she does as a parent. She wouldn't understand that I had particular needs that weren't met. I guess I learned that was not the kind of parent she could be to me and that's the reality of it.

Getting to college, though, was an entirely different world than the one I had known for the first 18 years of my life. I went to the furthest school I could find in the state: East Carolina University. I always thought about going to school in Virginia, but the cost of tuition out there quickly said, "Hell no!" So East Carolina was our winner! I chose the furthest school I could, away from my family, away from people at my high school- *on purpose*. I wanted to know how to grow up and learn things on my own and I wanted to make sure that none of them could ever come see me, as the school was almost six hours away. What's sad is that I wasn't even completely sold on the idea of college, and I was far from being in love with the idea, but I wanted to separate myself from the responsibilities that my family laid on me. Most of all, I wanted to learn how to be my own person. To my family, I was the "responsible kid," the one that "knew what she was doing," the one who seemingly always had everything together and who had to help take care of everyone.

My younger sister was hearing impaired, so she depended on me a lot, emotionally and for communication purposes in order to get through school. To add fuel to the fire, I had my mom who had an unhappy marriage, with a husband who couldn't be a husband or a dad. I was forced to bear that responsibility of not being a problem kid because they already had a problematic marriage. I had two biological parents who wanted nothing to do with me and grandparents who weren't healthy. I had brothers and sisters who I knew nothing about and uncles who weren't reliable, so I was like, "You know what seems peaceful? Independence! I'm getting out on my own and if I have to struggle, I'll struggle."

My family even blamed me for my sister going downhill. They said, "You're not here to help her. You're not here anymore. You kept her together and you're no longer here." I replied, completely shocked, "I'm only 18 years old. How dare you act like it is my job to be my sister's parent." To this day, I feel like they blame me for it. She still isn't doing well, emotionally, not that she ever had been, but I was that thing that kept her together. But then I decided to completely remove myself from my family. For the first time in my life, I chose me. I couldn't continue worrying and caring for everyone else except myself. Finally, I had an opportunity to focus on me, my life and where I was headed. I came home maybe twice a year from college and only a few people heard from me at all. For the few times I did go home, it was a bit of a strange experience. It's like, your parents are trying to adjust to these new versions of you as you're trying to discover who you are. A lot of us are met with such resistance, when discovering who we are because our parents are constantly comparing us to who we were when we lived with them and then you're only home long enough to say "Hey" then leave. They don't even have time to process what they see and then you come home and you're a little more different each time. That was, unfortunately, their process with me.

I was coming home every six months, a little different. It was like, "I'm a little more into philosophy now, I want to learn a little more about science now." *Hell, I even went vegan!* As you might imagine, that didn't go over too well with my very southern mother. She often conflated my newfound veganism with me simply not wanting to eat her cooking anymore. To hear me say that I no longer wanted any of her prized macaroni and cheese casserole was a stab to the heart for her. *I kid you not.* For two years, my mom held this grudge against me because she thought I had something against her cooking. I tried to explain it to her, saying, “Mom, we have cancer in this family, and I found out that some of it might be prevented if we take precautions so I’m going to change my diet.” Unsurprisingly, she replied, “It’s my food! You don’t want my fried chicken anymore!” I was like, “I want my arteries when I’m 60!” Now that some years have passed, she’s had some time to come around. Nowadays, she will happily reiterate her doctor’s advice of “incorporating more vegetables in your diet." Yeah, because a little cauliflower never hurt anyone.

I will say, though, it's been fascinating going through all of that change and discovering that I love change. Funny enough, I realized quickly that I had no social skills when I went to college because, to be honest, I had been such a hermit for most of my life. In high school, I did all of the sports and clubs, but I was quiet. I didn't rock boats. I did what I was told and then I would leave. Now, all of sudden, I had received this new lease on freedom, and I had to talk to people and make decisions. I was like, "You mean I have to go out there and talk to these strangers outside my dormitory...on purpose?" I always waited for an extrovert to come adopt me because that was the only way I was getting through the social anxiety I was experiencing. These extroverts were always pulling me into different spaces, spaces I wouldn't have ordinarily been in. It was a series of meeting new people, adjusting to their ways of being and, unintentionally, learning so much more about myself.

I encountered this one guy during my orientation, and I started hanging out with him and his friends. But of course, I noticed that I was the outsider coming in. I was friends with him, but not with his friends. I also ended up meeting someone in my dorm who was extroverted, but she liked parties. Guess who cared less for these parties? *Me!* Ultimately, I had these different friend groups, but I wasn't friends with any of them; I was navigating meeting people, knowing that I likely wouldn't be talking to them in a month. It was a revolving door of people coming into my life and leaving in what seemed like an instant. But then there came a moment, a glorious moment that changed everything and I never saw it coming.

During my Spanish class, I found out that there were salsa lessons being offered from a guy from out of town who would come and teach once a month. One day, I decided that I would give it a shot. It was new and something that had piqued my interest for some reason. I'm glad I went that day because that is where I found my social skills, that is where I began connecting with others in a way I had never done before. I never danced growing up, but that certainly didn't stop me from trying. To put it plainly: I loved salsa! Everyone would be dancing, I was being social, but I didn't have to talk to anyone. It was perfect for me. To this day, that's why I love to dance. You can imagine my frustration when I encounter those salsa partners who want to talk and they're like, "Hey! How's it going? How are you...etc." In my mind, I'm typically thinking, "I didn't come here for the small talk. I came in here and my social battery was at 60; don't bring me down to 30 in this conversation." Discovering dance opened up a whole new world for me, meeting new people and making connections with people that I had more in common with than my previous friends. But just as college was a great time, as far as me finding myself, it was also full of some of my darkest moments.

There's about a full year missing from my memory of my time in college. I was in a relationship during my second year of college with this guy who did not go to college with me. We crossed paths at a salsa event that he happened to be hosting at a local bar. He was from Mexico, taking care of his family and he didn't have a great home life either. He felt responsible for his family and at that particular time, it was apparent that he cared more about work than the people around him. He was a workaholic. He was the type of guy to make Valentine's Day plans with you, but also be working throughout the entire date. He was neglectful in general and being the passive aggressive person that I was at that time, I didn't know how to vocalize that my needs were not being met, but there came a moment when something happened between us. To this day, I can't tell you what exactly happened. He did something to me, but I have no memory of it. I know that it was the most devastating time in my life. I know I got to a place where I wanted to die and I was beginning to think of ways to make it happen, including driving my car off a bridge and I wouldn't have cared at all. I told myself, "It would've been my time to go." These thoughts had me so shaken that I decided that it was time for me to go back to therapy and I stayed in therapy until I graduated.

It wasn't just the incident that I could barely recall; I barely remember half of my time in therapy. Interestingly enough, I met up with him years later and he kept apologizing for whatever happened. I looked at him and said, "Everyone seems to know what happened to me. I don't know what you did, but you have to live with that guilt. I don't want to know." He knows what happened, his friends know and even my mom knows, but I told her not to tell me. People were asking him, "She didn't murder you on site?! Wow, you are lucky!" My assumption is that at least part of what he did included sexual assault because I have faint memories of strange things happening while he was drunk, but that's it. I barely remember life with him or even living with him. But while I can't recall that time period in college, I can tell you that I was flunking my classes with flying colors. I barely graduated college because I was flunking my entire junior year. The depression and suicidal thoughts were too much. The pain was unrelenting, and it felt like there was no escaping it. But therapy helped me to get to the heart of a lot of my issues.

I remember my therapist telling me how passive aggressive I came off. He mentioned how it doesn't solve anything and how I needed to learn how to assert myself. At first, I couldn't see what he was talking about, but I had also never realized that I wasn't the best at sticking up for myself. I wasn't the type to confront my problems; running from them was easier. More so, my therapist helped connect the pieces of who I am and why I am the way I am. He said, "You had an enabling mother who used you as an emotional support child, you had biological parents who didn't want you, you had your typical abandonment issues from your dad, and you learned to keep your head down and not ask questions. You got into this relationship with this guy, and you continue to do the same thing and then you hit a wall. What did you think you were going to do? Continue to take it?" I was speechless. Suddenly, it all made sense in some strange way. I knew he was right. I was grateful for that year and a half of therapy. I do not think I would've finished college without it.

I know that in the black community, mental health isn't exactly a favorable topic of discussion, but I think people need to be more transparent about the fact that we all have issues and those of us that have been to therapy need to be honest about what we got from it. I think when we all keep secrets, we all put it under the rug or put it in the closet and never deal with it. We like the idea of seeming strong because it makes us feel better, but none of us like feeling vulnerable. No one wants to admit that we're crying at home every day. I'm in therapy now, and my mom is seeing the change in me; she mentions it all the time now, but when I first went to therapy and I would talk to her about it, she would say, "We don't have problems in this family." Or perhaps she would utilize the more infamous saying, you know, that typical black response of "No one has depression, no one has any mental health issues in this family, I don't know what you're talking about." You know, "I'm fine." I honestly think it's a lack of transparency. No one wants to admit that we're not okay because then we're seen as weak and none of us want to be weak because society already makes us feel weak. However, working on one's own mental health often means confronting yourself in every possible way. As fate would have it, aside from processing the fallout from my traumatic experience from the guy that left me depressed and suicidal, I also needed to begin processing another part of myself that I had buried long ago: my interest in women.

Honestly, It was hard realizing that I liked girls, but it was a realization that was more than necessary. When I finally left my parents' house, I realized that I had suppressed so much of my emotions as a kid. By the time college rolled around, I was strongly against dating, but something weird began to happen when I got there: I began having dreams about women. However, a year and half passed before I acknowledged it out loud. I was with my first boyfriend at the time, and I told him, "Hey. I might like girls, but I don't know." When he asked why I thought that I may be into women, I said, "Well I keep having these consistent dreams of these girls touching me and it's making me question everything!"

And of course, being the man he was, he ended up setting up a threesome for us. That option was more comfortable to me then because I didn't want to be left alone in a room with a woman, so I was like, *"Great!"* I welcomed the threesome, which was with one of his best friends. I knew immediately that I liked it, but my brain completely blocked it and said, "You're going to continue to date men for the next five years anyway!" But by the time I graduated college, I was going to gay clubs and beginning to express myself more and more. There was only one gay bar in my college town, and I partied hard there! If it wasn't for that gay bar, then I don't know what I would've done. I get why, for some queer people, our go-to place is the club. It's a place to escape, people who won't judge us, and it helps us forget. I totally understand how that can be our first instinct- to go to the bars.

Due to my social anxiety, I drove past that bar a few times, then I'd park and go home. Sometimes, I'd park, see how much it cost to get in and then leave. When I finally went in, I didn't talk to or dance with anyone. As time went on, I had visited so often and partied so hard, that they knew me by name. I had gotten free CDs because I was there dancing the entire time, up until they closed for the night. This went on for a while, but I eventually graduated, got a job, and at the end of my last relationship with a guy, the feelings for women kept coming back. I had dated men, women, been at salsa socials, dancing all over and making out with everybody. While I'm not the biggest fan of labels, I know that I'm queer and proud of it. I've experienced sincere joy in companionship with women and men so who knows what the future has for me in that area. But as crazy as this journey has been, I don't know if I would change it. I think I can say that I'm learning to find peace within myself, who I am, and where I'm headed in life. For me, part of finding this peace meant exploring different avenues that I had never considered before.

Two years ago, I went down a spiritual journey, exploring various religious paths, including working with a few Muslim women, and learning all that they had to offer. For a year, I explored Islam, even covering my hair and it changed my life. I dressed a lot more modestly and I was at the mosque a lot. It was an eye-opening experience, listening to Imams and priests and all of these people from these religious backgrounds and getting their perspectives on not only their specific religion, but mostly life. In my time studying Islam, I found that people had to look me in my face and not my hair since it was covered. For the first time, I felt respected. It was fascinating. In turn, I also felt like my energy was being protected. After a year, I decided to keep covering my hair, but I never officially converted to Islam or any other specific religion. Covering my hair feels like a shield from other people's energies; I can keep my own energy and stay grounded this way. I tried walking out without my scarf covering my hair and I couldn't do It. I don't wear it when I dance, but I wear it everywhere else now.

Even with all of this though, I don't know if I ever want to fully live by a specific religious doctrine. I guess you could say I'm more into honing into my spirituality. Incense, my spiritual guides, tarot cards, and crystals are what I'm into. I was telling my therapist a few weeks ago that I'm finally figuring out how to live. I've taken different avenues to figure out who I am and all I could come to is that I'm a nurturer, I'm sensitive, a survivor, resilient, caring, a little chaotic in energy, a little dramatic but happy with it, but also, I can be serious. I can be in my head a bit too much, but I like that. I'm a jack of all trades, but master of none; that is the essence of who I am- wanting to take in everything.

As I begin looking towards the future, I see myself causing trouble in the middle of Switzerland somewhere and accepting my lack of wanting to conform my mind. I'm going to be chaotic to any company, friends, or job. I'm going to be the person coming in with conflict because I'm willing to challenge it, challenge the status quo. I want to throw myself in the middle of nowhere and cause trouble- *good trouble*- without even trying to. I can't see myself doing something I don't want to, like teaching, even though I'd probably be good at it. But if I've learned nothing else over the course of my journey, it is that to get to where you want to be, in whatever fashion, you have to be able to accept being emotionally alone.

If you can't be alone with yourself and realize that people around you will not understand every part of your journey, then you will not get to where you want to be. You won't be happy with yourself. There's that sacrifice of knowing that whatever I do, people may not get it, but it's not about them getting it, it's about you getting it and you have to be okay with them not getting it for a while before they respect it. Too many people are afraid of being alone and being different. It's hard but discovering who you are as a person is always more important than making other people comfortable. Always remember that.

Not So Fun Fact: Black women disproportionately experience violence at home, at school, on the job, and in their neighborhoods. For every black woman who reports rape, at least 15 black women do not report.

- **One in four black girls will be sexually abused before the age of 18.**
- **One in five black women are survivors of rape.**
- **Thirty-five percent of black women experienced some form of contact sexual violence during their lifetime.**
- **Forty to sixty percent of black women report being subjected to coercive sexual contact by age 18.**

-The National Center on Violence Against Women in the Black Community (2018)

It's Sad Outside

Derrick's Story

He/Him

In my household, as a child, it was your typical mother, father and 2.5 kids, but it was dysfunctional. I am one of two children, originally from Boston, but I grew up in Marietta, Georgia. My father was an alcoholic, (*though he is recovered now)* so not only did my mom have to deal with taking care of her two kids, but she also had to manage everything with my father, too. I was pretty sure that she was superwoman. However, no matter how powerful my mom may have been, she couldn't save me from the anxiety I started to feel as a result of the constant dysfunction in the household.

I think I started to experience anxiety as early as seven years old, which was when we moved to Georgia from Boston. It was only my parents, my sister and I that lived in Georgia. We didn't have anyone else here at the time. Even though my mom was always there, my sister was almost like a second mom to me growing up. She's nine years older than me so she was in high school when we moved. She says that things were crazy before we moved to Georgia, but I can't remember because I was so young. But, as an adult, I can see how so many things from our childhood have impacted both her and I.

Dealing with anxiety at such a young age, I didn't know what to do. I was always full of fear, and I didn't like for things to be out of order. I liked a consistent schedule, which has translated into my dull life now. *Ha-ha!* I needed consistency. I noticed that I stayed to myself because I didn't want to rock the boat, so I internalized a lot. It was already rocky due to my dad, and I had a lot of fear due to everything going on. My mom was a rock for my sister and I during that time. I was always a mama's boy and I think she did a good job at trying to shield me and my sister from seeing different things. She wanted to give us everything. Honestly, me and my sister were pretty spoiled kids. My mom made sure we had the coolest clothes and gadgets, trying to deter the attention from my dad.

While there was some dysfunction within our house, I found that it was a common theme throughout our family because I would see similar dysfunction at other relative's homes when the rest of my mom's side of the family moved from Boston to Atlanta a year or two later. The dysfunction had been an ongoing cycle that had lasted through several generations. It was like we had more support and I had met friends by this time, but it wasn't exactly a relief to go visit family because there were similar problems. By the time I got to middle school, things were worse in my own home.

During this time, my sister had gotten pregnant with my niece and my dad was far from supportive of that. Fortunately, my mom fought to support her, deciding that she would be there for my sister and my niece: that decision ignited the tension in the household. My dad could have chosen to be supportive, but he didn't. So, as I'm going through puberty, already navigating all of these new hormones, my anxiety worsened due to everything going on in the house without much of any outlet for it, so I started binge eating to cope. I was anxious all the time because I was so uncomfortable all the time, which also led me to begin cutting myself, too.

They used to say that the sitcom, *Degrassi*, was great because we were learning about other kids that are going through the same thing that we're going through. But I didn't know what cutting was before I watched *Degrassi*. I learned, "Oh, if you cut yourself, then you can feel relief." So that's what I started doing. That's how I let out all my frustration because I didn't know how to ask for help or that I was supposed to ask for help from my parents. The cutting and binge eating lasted through the full nine months that my sister was pregnant because it was a crazy time. My dad was angry all the time and my mom was trying to keep the peace. I wouldn't say that I did it every day, but every other day maybe, I would cut, and binge eat. I guess when my niece was born, that's when the cutting and binge eating stopped. I think I had a new thing to focus on, helping my sister take care of my niece. It was a distraction.

As far as my anxiety, it was still heightened, except for maybe when I was holding the baby. I still had a lot of anxiety, but I wouldn't necessarily act on it negatively towards myself; I would redirect my energy. There was still a lot of fighting in the household. My dad despised my niece's father so that caused a lot of tension that didn't need to be there. I think for the first couple of months after my niece was born, the depression and anxiety subsided, but then after a while it started to come back. I didn't cut or anything, but I went with the flow, and I think I distracted myself with video games as well since that was around the time I got my Xbox.

Also, I guess you could say that during this time, in middle school, was when I realized that I was a bit different when compared to the other boys, realizing, "Oh, I think I like boys." Realizing that I was gay, or bisexual wasn't a huge part of why I felt anxious, though. I don't know if I blocked it out or thought that it wouldn't matter, but it didn't make me more anxious at all. Of course, I had moments where I thought that if I weren't gay, that'd be one less thing I have to worry about. Sometimes, I would try to change my brain, like specifically watching lesbian porn in order to rewire my thoughts. Almost like, "I am going to like this!" But I didn't dwell on it at all. I kept it all to myself and didn't focus on it. I came out when I was 16 years old, with two of my best friends and a cousin being the first I told. They all replied with, "I know already." With me thinking, "Damn! What was I doing that made it so obvious? I clearly didn't do a good job at hiding it."

Most of my anxiety towards my sexuality, as minimal as it was, was at school. I was anxious about hiding myself so I wouldn't be called a faggot, even though in my senior year, a boy screamed out that I was faggot anyway. And of course, I was always a little more on edge when I was around boys that I possibly had a crush on. (*But then again, who doesn't get a little anxious when their crush is talking to them*). I wish I could say that things started to look up from there, but unfortunately, that wasn't the case. My sister moved back to Massachusetts to move in with her dad when I was 13 years old.

When she left, it was less anxiety and more depression that I was experiencing. We were always so close. In 8th grade and some of 9th grade, I was depressed all the time. My niece's sperm donor was a horrible person, so my sister had to get away. To save her and my niece's life, she had to go live with her dad in Boston. I had to find a new normal, a normal without the physical presence and support of my sister, who has always been one of my best friends. Now, it was only me and my parents living in the house and that wasn't the ideal situation. By the time I turned 18 years old and went off to college, my parents had divorced and went their separate ways for good. I knew it was coming, but it kinda rattled me: it fucked me up. I thought they should've done it years ago, but I guess better late than never. I was graduating high school and my life was changing. My mom was moving to one place and my dad was moving to another. It was too much at once. Fortunately, I was going off to college and I had my own set of challenges there that needed my attention.

I initially went to Southern Polytechnic State University, which I picked because it was close to home. I tried to not make myself feel like my whole life wasn't crumbling down so I didn't go far for college, staying in my own backyard of Marietta, Georgia. I went there for a year, thinking I wanted to do computer science because I liked doing HTML on Myspace. But I soon learned that they weren't the same. So, after realizing that I probably shouldn't be at a technology school, I transferred to Georgia State University and instantly regretted that decision. I hated it mostly because I didn't get the community feel down there; I felt alone even around so many people. I was commuting because I couldn't afford to live on campus, which only made the feeling of isolation worse. To add the cherry on top, I was dating this guy who was the definition of toxic. One of our last big arguments was about some guy adding me on Twitter, with the argument ending with him saying, “Fuck you! I’m gonna leave you…” blah blah blah. *Complete bullshit.*

At that point, I saw that I was at a school that I wasn’t comfortable at, my mom had lost her job, so things were tight around the house, and my dad was in North Carolina and at the height of his addiction. All of this was happening at the same time. Something in my brain asked, “What did you do to feel good when you last felt like this? Cut.” So, one day, I went into the kitchen, and I took a butcher knife and stabbed myself in my arm and I made two huge cuts. I thought that this would be the moment I bleed out. I blacked out, to be honest. I don’t know if I was trying to commit suicide or if I was trying to feel relief. But immediately I thought,

"*What the fuck did I just do?!*" I was so embarrassed with myself that I didn't go to the emergency room, even though I probably should have. I went to CVS and picked up everything I could to make it heal. I tried to cover it up, but the unfortunate thing about covering up two huge marks on your arm in the summertime in Georgia is that you can't cover it up, especially walking in downtown Atlanta.

My mom saw it and told me that I needed to get help and talk to someone because it wasn't okay. I ended up reaching out to GA State counseling services. After the initial consultation and them realizing that I self-harmed pretty badly, they got me in ASAP to see a therapist. At 19 years old, I was in therapy for the first time, and it felt good. I was only in therapy for a semester, but I was able to do some good work. I was coming into understanding myself as a person and knowing what I needed to do to be okay in general. After therapy, I realized that I was done with GA State University. They helped me with counseling services, but it wasn't the best fit for me, so I transferred to Kennesaw State University (KSU) soon after and then the sky opened up. I felt like I was part of a community, I knew people and met people easier, and it was right in my backyard, with me growing up right down from the school. The campus made the difference. When you went to KSU, there was a campus where all the buildings and people were in one area. You got to see people around, but with GA State, you were mixed in with the people who were headed to work, students and the city overall.

I didn't consider continuing counseling services at KSU because I was in a pink cloud, doing something new and it felt good; I felt like I had a new lease on life. Nothing about my life changed, except the school I was going to. I was in this space of everything feeling good. Also, I transferred to KSU in the summer, which is important because I suffer from seasonal affective disorder. When I transferred to KSU, it was all rainbows and sunlight; I was happy there. For those that don't know, Seasonal Affective Disorder is when your mood is elevated in the summer and spring months but decreases in the winter and fall months. My mom says that even at three years old, I would say, "Mom, it's sad outside," during the winter months. So, I think, even from a young age, I dealt with it, but I didn't know it and neither did my parents. I got that diagnosis recently from my therapist. Although I suspected that I had it long before, the actual diagnosis came recently, in 2020, to be specific. But KSU, as a whole, was a much better experience for me and it seemed like new doors were opening for me.

I entered KSU, majoring in Spanish education, but I ended up graduating with a bachelor's in integrated studies/Spanish and Leadership. In high school, I loved to go to Spanish class so in college, I started taking Spanish again. *(Fun fact: I'm not the best test-taker so I bombed the AP Spanish test in high school).* Even at the height of my depression and anxiety at 19 years old, nothing mattered when I was in that class. I felt good there, which is why I changed majors. I thought I would become an interpreter for the Department of Family and Children Services (DFCS) and possibly teaching, since we have a huge population of Hispanic people in the area that needed help. I wanted to do that, but that ended up not working out. While things were looking up as far as my education, my love life got a boost at KSU as well.

I got to KSU that summer and at the end of the summer, I broke up with my ex-boyfriend. Around fall 2012, *(my first real semester at KSU)*, that's when I met Kyle. We actually met on *Okcupid*. If you let him tell the story, then he would tell you that he thought I was being thirsty because I sent two messages and sent my phone number too. I didn't even get on the app like that, and I was newly single; I was ready to hit the streets and be crazy. *Keep in mind that Grindr was out at that time, too*. I had a Grindr account, and I was ready to be a hoe. But that didn't happen. *Tragic.* Luckily, we're still together to this day.

I graduated from KSU in December 2014 and after graduating, I immediately took a job at GA

State University, which is pretty ironic because I hated my time there as a student. I don't know why I thought I would like to work there. I worked there for six months, commuting from Kennesaw to downtown Atlanta every day. My car was fucking up and they weren't paying enough. It wasn't all about money, but I was trying to survive! In fact, I was working there and working a second job at *LensCrafters*. It was crazy and I knew something had to give. I knew that I had to find something closer to home because aside from my car breaking down, it wasn't the best environment for me to work in. Also, I was tired of working two jobs and I was living on my own with Kyle and a roommate; there was a lot happening at once.

Nowadays, nearly seven years after graduating, I work as a sales rep and I'm moving into real estate, too. I take my licensure test for real estate in early April, but I still have to finish my courses. The program is 75 hours, but you go at your own pace, so it all depends on how fast you're able to work through it, but I'm honestly happy that I've made it this far. I've learned that as far as mental health is concerned; you have to keep working at it. In 2019 and 2020, I had a hard time with myself. I was severely depressed. Like, off the charts depressed. During that time, I was dealing with family issues that stemmed from 2016. Also, for a long period of my life, *(maybe 2016-2019),* I would try to do things to make myself feel better, like working out but I was never serious about it. I also picked up the habit of drinking to manage my anxiety and depression and it honestly made it worse. It was a domino effect.

After those three and half years of doing all the wrong things, I got to a point where I couldn't take it anymore. I was working hard, got all my debt paid off, even bought a house. I thought I should feel good, but I still wasn't happy. I was distracting myself by accomplishing all those things. Now I was at this point where I got all the things I was working towards, but I was still fucking depressed. That's when I knew it was time to go back to therapy. That's when I realized that managing my mental health is an on-going process. It's an on-going struggle.

You may never rid yourself of depression or anxiety completely, but you can work to make your life a bit better every day. You have to keep doing the work even once you're happy and feeling better; you have to stay on top of your mental health. It'll help you stay strong. I'm still in therapy now, though I'm down from meeting weekly and bi-weekly to monthly. But I'm doing a lot better. It keeps me accountable. If I were to keep doing bi-weekly sessions, then I don't feel as though it would give me the incentive to do the work that I need to do, to become a better person and manage my depression on my own. So, it's important to do the work in the month time frame and talk it over with my therapist and everything seems good. For anyone that's dealing with any type of mental health issue, it is important to be patient with yourself because every day is going to be different and it may be a constant battle for you, but things do get better.

Not So Fun Fact : According to the Centers for Disease Control and Prevention (CDC), suicide is the third leading cause of death for black males, ages 15-24. Suicide rates have doubled among black men since 1980.

-Centers for Disease Control and Prevention (2019)

The Good Daughter

Lydia's Story

She/Her

Life is pretty funny sometimes. Right before I got here to speak with you, I was telling my ex, "I'm about to go do an interview for mental health" and he looked at me (*keep in mind that I dated this man for almost two years)* and said, "Wait, you have mental health issues?" I looked at him like, "I know you fuckin' lying!" What was so crazy is that he has seen me at my low points, including during my depressive episodes and anxiety. I know I'm pretty high functioning with my anxiety, but he's seen me at my worst, bawling my eyes out, unable to move. Like, *What do you mean, "You have mental health issues?!"* He responded, generalizing it by saying, "Yeah, but I mean everyone gets a little wound up." I wanted to go into more detail with him, but I knew it would only end in an argument. In fact, the decline in my mental health is the reason I broke up with him.

Towards the end of our relationship, I didn't know where I stood with him anymore. I didn't know if we were still together or not, and it messed with my head. We weren't even talking much, so it even had me wondering if he was cheating or wondering if I wasn't doing enough. I could always feel the anxiety that I was experiencing over the status of this relationship, and the fact that he didn't even seem to notice made everything worse. Also, at the time, I had a death in the family and needed a lot of love and support from him, which I didn't get. After losing her husband, my aunt needed me to be there for her, but I was preoccupied with my own relationship issues; I wasn't even happy within myself. I ended up shoving everything down so I could be there for her, suppressing my own pain. He wasn't there for me, and I kept asking myself, "How can you be in a relationship with someone, and your partner isn't giving you what you need, although you're giving them what they need?" That's neglect and I told him that. He said that he never thought of it that way, but I guess that doesn't really matter now since we're not together.

At least I can say that I was honest with him and told him that he was messing with my mental health. I mean, I was completely fixating on him, with thoughts like, "Am I going to see him this week or not?" I couldn't let go, but I've also come to learn that I have control issues. Funny enough, when I broke up with him, it didn't make my feelings any better because I wanted him to fight for me- *and he didn't*. It messed with my self-esteem, and I had an intense episode of having these thoughts of, "Why didn't he love me enough? What could I have done?" while also telling myself, "There's nothing else you could've done." During this episode, there were literally moments where, for every negative thought, I would try to create a positive thought to combat it. I found myself sitting in the middle of my bed, begging the thoughts to stop, and reminding myself to breathe, looking at my door hoping that none of my brothers or anyone would walk through the door and see me like this. I tried to muffle my cries while also trying to breathe and ended up falling asleep, only to wake up and wonder, "What just happened?"

This last relationship made me realize how bad things can get if you don't take care of yourself. In fact, all of the issues I had while growing up, including issues with my family, showed up in my last relationship. Dating this person after six years of singleness, suddenly brought up so many issues that I had believed were gone up until that point; I thought I was fine. I found out I was lying to myself- *and Jesus.* In the past, I would've told you that I hadn't experienced anything with mental health until I began college. I can look back, now, and see that I've always struggled with issues with hyperventilating, loss of time, and my mind being too overwhelmed with thoughts to the point of breaking down. I always thought, not that I was weak, but that I wasn't strong enough to handle everything or that I was being too much of a perfectionist.

By the time I entered college, the mixture of paperwork, the pressure to be a good daughter, good sibling, good worker, good student, and good to everybody as a whole, left me completely neglecting myself. I would go months without noticing that I was going through the days, and weeks without eating or caring for myself in any meaningful way. Due to the amount of pressure I was under, often self-inflicted, I would even forget what month or day it was sometimes. Now that I'm a bit older and more self-aware, I realize that it wasn't good at all, but I didn't have the language then to verbalize what was going on with me. I felt like I didn't have someone to lean on, although I was that someone for everyone. It was like every time I would try to express myself, everyone was like, "Oh, it's just college! This is normal. You're fine!" But the problem is that when you're always "fine," everyone thinks you're simply having a bad moment when, in actuality, you're not fine.

With all of this said, it is crystal clear to me that much of this, most of my problems, are rooted in my upbringing and the complicated nature of it all. Growing up in a Jamaican household, my parents were hard on me and since they expected perfection from me then, I expected it from myself through college and beyond. I was doing what I was trained to do so I seek perfection in every aspect of my life and when I don't get it, I don't deal well. I internalize it as me being the problem, 24/7. My family never directly called me a failure, but I felt like I was when I did not excel. I pushed myself too hard in many instances and sometimes I really had some tough thoughts like, "You're a fuckin' failure." I know my parents and the rest of my family love me, but in many cases, the pressure was just too much.

My parents divorced when I was young, and I can't even tell you when they actually divorced because I can only ever remember them being separated. Their wedding book is the only "memory" I have of them being together. My mom married my step-dad when I was in elementary school, so I never felt like I was raised in a broken home or anything like that. I did, however, feel like there were things that weren't available to me because my mom has always been this person who is tight with money so I would always ensure I didn't ask for certain things or even go places with friends because I didn't want to be a burden on her. I always felt like it was me being selfish, especially since at that time, there were about seven people in the house: me, my sister, my three brothers, my mom and step-dad. So, I never asked for anything. They say the middle child gets overlooked, but I never felt overlooked; I tried to be the kid that didn't have problems or cause any problems. When I did have problems, I tried to be the kid that handled them myself so I wouldn't become a problem to my family. With my mom, I felt like I had to conform to her expectations and whatever she wanted from me. That conformity and the need to do everything that was expected of me from her and other family members *(because everyone had high expectations for me)* played into my anxiety. The feelings of inadequacy and feeling like I wasn't enough were always omnipresent in a way.

I can even remember one night in particular where we went to an award ceremony in high school and I received all of these different kinds of awards, but I didn't make honors. I think I had a 3.48 GPA, which was still great, but it didn't meet the level of success that my family was expecting.

After receiving all of these other awards and gaining recognition in other areas, my grandma looked at me and said, “But you didn’t make honors?” I’m standing there with all of these awards and all of these people are saying nice things about me and she’s looking at me like I failed. It crushed me and it made me feel so inadequate. Because I wasn’t up there with those who made honors, it completely overshadowed everything else I had done. All the things I did throughout high school like recycling, French club, and winning most spirited- it was all worthless, in her eyes. Because I didn’t have that one little stole for honors, none of it mattered to her. Currently, as I’m embarking on my second degree, I still haven’t gotten past the fact that I can’t fail due to possible familial retribution or disappointment.

Also, I found that my family placing me on a pedestal and comparing my brothers to me didn't help either. The bar was set much higher for me and I experience a new low every time I "fail" at something. When I feel like I've fallen short, I can feel the disappointment in my family; it's almost as if I've failed them as well, almost as if they're saying, "How dare you?!" As a matter of fact, this past Wednesday, I was at my clinicals. I was working on an assignment, but then the nurse I was working with made the comment, "You're headed in the right direction, but not really." I felt like I was doing good prior to her saying that, especially because we had so many assignments that were already due this past week. I immediately went into the bathroom and started crying. I began looking at myself in the mirror and telling myself, "You're not a failure. One little hitch isn't that bad. You can redo it. You're fine!"

I wiped my face and pulled myself together before going back out because I didn't want people to baby me, which is a bit ironic because I always want someone to care. In the end, I walked out of the bathroom and still ended up crying on another nurse's scrubs for 10 or 15 minutes in the middle of the hall. I will say, though, I'll never forget the encouraging words that the nurse told me that day. The nurse said, "Let me tell you something, I learned how important it is to not speak negatively of your soul because you believe it." He told me that he could tell that I haven't been taking care of my anxiety. He said, "You have to stop trying to control everything," and I know he's right.

What's interesting, is that, at work, I've been told that I come off as someone who is rude for not giving a fuck or for standing up for myself to patients who want to be disrespectful, to doctors that want to be disrespectful, and acting in the best interest of my patients and not the company. Obviously, I'm not breaking HIPAA and OSHA laws, but I'm going to act in the best interest of my patient. I'm not rude, but over the years, I've been the person who didn't speak up for myself in fear of not being accepted. I've spent my life trying to not offend people because I was afraid of losing them; I always filtered what I wanted to say for momentary acceptance. I'm at the place in my life where I'm beginning to speak my mind and if you don't like it...well...we only work together. *Now, if only I could keep that same energy with family and friends- I'd be top tier!*

But even with this new mindset, my anxiety can still be crippling. Normally, when I get bad anxiety, it's because I get stressed and end up putting more on my plate than I can handle. With my stress, if I haven't had a good cry- *a big release*- then one is most certainly coming, and it doesn't stop. It can last all day, or a few days and I don't know what that does for me. I think to myself sometimes that maybe crying is a form of therapy for me. I know I shouldn't overload myself in the first place, but I usually feel better after crying. It's hard to notice sometimes because I hold a lot in. What makes it even harder are the comments from my family. They're always like, "Well Lydia, you already got one degree before. You're fine." And I happily remind them that this is a master's degree and much more difficult than my bachelor's. My undergraduate degree is actually in Exercise Science (*because I wanted to be a physician's assistant at the time, but I didn't get accepted anywhere*), but the program I'm in now is an accelerated nursing program.

My first semester in nursing school, I found myself crying on my teacher's scrubs in class because I was so stressed out. She pulled me aside and said, "You need to understand what grace is. I can tell when someone is going to be a good nurse. You're going to be an exceptional nurse. You're going to be fine. You need to start giving yourself some grace or you're not going to make it." Now every time someone mentions the word "grace," I hear her voice. I low key wanted her to be my therapist. *Ha-ha!* She's a maternity nurse and has such a soothing voice. She gave me her phone number to use if I ever needed anything and, in my mind, I was like, "Sis, you don't know what you did!" So, every time she'd mention grace, I say to myself, "Lydia, you've gotten yourself out of some bad situations and it's important to list your accomplishments, even the seemingly minor ones. As a black female, I have one degree and now I'm moving on to getting a second one, holding down a job for a good six years. I'm well-versed in working in insurance, being a medical assistant, and I've gained a ton of skills. Be glad about what you have and don't compare yourself to anyone else." I'm always trying to work on myself, not only for my own sake, but I also try to be there for others as well.

My friend, who is in nursing school with me, has depression and anxiety and I feel like I try to take some of the burden off of her, so I don't have to tell her what I'm going through. I feel like our pain isn't equal, in the sense that what I'm going through isn't as bad as what she's going through. In my efforts of trying not to be a burden onto others, everything ends up building up inside of me. I've tried journaling, but it doesn't work for me even though it works for other people. Honestly, and this might sound funny, but journaling makes me think of *Moesha*. It hasn't been as therapeutic for me as it has for others, but I know it's not a one size fits all; I still try though! One of my friends suggested that I write something down every day, even positive affirmations for myself, but all I can think is how I could be studying an entire chapter for school instead. Somewhere along the line, I thought I'd give therapy a chance, but that didn't exactly go as planned.

I went to therapy once while I was at university. I thought it'd be a good idea to try the counseling services there since my tuition covered a few sessions; it was a disappointment to say the least. The therapist told me, during this first and only session, "You're not depressed, and you don't have anxiety. I feel like you're having detachment issues from your family, and you should take time to go see them." To put it into perspective, this was my second year at college, I was working two jobs- one during the week and one on the weekend- with a full class load. I was also in a few organizations at the same time, including being on the board for the International Students Association (ISA).

With all of this on my plate, I didn't see my family for nearly a month, and I usually see my brothers once a week/every other week or sometimes I'd drive up to see them and then drive right back. I couldn't do that anymore; I simply didn't have time. The therapist stated, "Your family is your support system. That's all you need, and you'll be fine." To be real with you, I was shocked. She said all this over one session and I felt like she wasn't listening to my problems, making assumptions based on what she heard during that first session, so I didn't go back. I didn't even want to go to therapy and only decided to give it a try because my boss, at that time, told me I should. She noticed that I wasn't talking to people *(and I talked a lot).* But it was evident that the therapist was not understanding where I was coming from. She didn't even give me any kind of assistance; not even something like breathing exercises. Instead, she led me to believe that it was all in my head. I told her how I'd sit on the floor in my room, telling myself, "Control your thoughts! Control your thoughts! Stop thinking of things all at one time. Stop! Stop! Stop!" and her response was that I was missing my family?

To this day, I still haven't found a fix. I've realized that my anxiety is in every aspect of my life, and I never noticed. It would even show up while I was at work, going into work crying, even to patients sometimes, knowing that it should probably be the other way around. I would go to work and be unhappy. I would feel like home was an unhappy place or that my relationship was an unhappy place so then I eventually felt empty. I was worrying about everything, unable to control anything, but wanting to control everything. I had all of these feelings of inadequacy and not being where I'm "supposed" to be at my age. Hating the job but needing the job, while my family was putting me on a high pedestal, with high expectations. I felt like so much was expected of me from every avenue and like no one was giving a fuck about how I actually felt and caring about if I could actually handle the weight of it all.

I'm still in the process of learning different tricks and tools that help me manage my mental health. I've been through a lot of self-help therapies, like alcohol therapy, *(10/10 would **not** recommend)* but of course that didn't lead to anything productive or beneficial. Right now, I'm into aromatherapy/candles. One time, I lit one candle and something about that being the only light in the room was extremely calming. It also made me want to breathe and take in the smell. It was nice. With the help of candles, I am able to focus on something that makes me happy. It's not always fully effective the closer I get to a breakdown, but otherwise, I've found it to be helpful. Also, I've noticed that I post a lot of quotes on social media because, I think, it's either something I need to know, something that speaks to my spirit, something I needed to hear in the past or something that makes me feel like I'm not alone.

With that said, though, I also have to take breaks from social media for my mental health. The constant comparison of my life to others isn't healthy. In addition, much like candles and aromatherapy. I've found that music, especially R&B music, is soothing to me and it brings me joy. It could be a love song about somebody breaking up, but that beat be bussin! Music has always helped me, even when I'm studying. It helps me to not focus too hard on everything that's on my plate. Unfortunately for me, I'll work on my mental health and then I'll fall off, repeating that cycle over and over again. I'll typically feel like I'm at a good place and then I'll fall off, no longer participating in my self-care. I read things and try to have insight, which doesn't always lead to the desired result, but it has allowed more space for some self-reflection. Like, after my breakup with my ex, I wrote down some things that I needed to work on within myself in order to be good to myself and a future partner. One thing that I thought of was speaking my mind and stop being afraid that I would lose people for doing so.

Also, I realized that I needed to stop thinking I was a burden all the time and stop being vulnerable with people that don't deserve it. I will talk and connect with people, but I feel like God will put it on my spirit when some people simply aren't good for me. He lets me know when certain relationships aren't good for me, but when I know that I don't want to hear something *(because it'll conflict with my mind and my own desires)*, I talk to God less. It's avoidance. Realizing that, it's all about self-reflection, but only reflecting isn't enough: you have to apply. I'm at a place right now where I know I can't keep having crying fits or blocking people out. I have a friend that will ask if I'm okay and I always say I'm fine. She reminds me that, through text messages, I'll vent to her, but in person, I always say "I'm fine," even though I had been crying earlier. She thinks that I'm continuing to avoid and she's probably right, but I guess you can say that I'm a work in progress.

Ideally, in the future, I want to be at peace. I want to stop nitpicking at everything because my life is not how I thought it should be or continue operating on some societal timeline for my life. We gotta stop thinking that 30 is old or that life ends at 30. I have to stop obsessing over my age and what I see on social media, even what some of my friends' post. I'm blessed and that's something that I think I should keep in mind. Moving forward, there is so much that I want to be at peace with. I want to be at peace with the fact that, if I choose not to go back to my doctorate, my RN is still good enough. I want to be at peace with my body image as well in the future. Although it has never been loved or accepted by my family, it still has to be loved and accepted by me. I want to be comfortable and at peace with who I am as a person. If someone tells me something that they don't like about me, then that doesn't mean that I need to reevaluate who I am as a person. Just because one person doesn't like one thing about me doesn't mean I need to change. Also, I know that I have to stop pleasing people; I don't want to always conform to the thoughts and expectations of others.

I need to be at peace with my friends, enjoying my time with them, laughing, having movie nights, and enjoying drinking games. I want to be able to be vulnerable with people and I don't want to always have to compromise myself to do it. I want to get to a place of feeling worthy of loving myself, which includes my thick ass 4c hair, to my big ole stomach, loud mouth and attitude sometimes. I want to be okay with myself and at peace with where I am in life now. I'm hoping to get there one day. To anyone who may read this, know that you're not always the problem. There are things that people need to work on and make better about themselves. The only expectations that you need to follow are the ones, realistically, that you've set for yourself and not the other ones that people have placed on you. But also, get help when you need it. Find someone who you can confide in.

I learned recently that my little brother had depression in high school, but never felt comfortable expressing that to anyone, including me. He started crying during his 21st birthday celebration this year and I told him that he has to talk to someone, and he responded, "What if they leave?" I replied, "You're gonna have to take that risk, but you can't bottle it up. You're gonna have to judge who your friends are as people, but also find help so you're not keeping it all bottled up in your mind. Find someone who you can vent to without them trying to fix you unless you ask for their help. Find someone that doesn't make you feel like a burden, someone that makes you feel like you deserve to breathe this air that God has allowed you to." And reader, I'm extending that same message to you; make space for you and all that you are.

Not So Fun Fact: Because Blacks, particularly Black women, experience higher rates of depression than their White female or Black male counterparts but receive lower rates of adequate treatment, they remain one of the most undertreated groups in the United States.

-Psych Central (2016)

Poster Boy

River's Story

He/Him

For as long as I can remember, I always lived in this box. It was tall enough for me to stand and wide enough for me to lay down, but not an inch more. It was snug and volatile at the same time. I think it may have been impenetrable from both sides. For what seemed like an eternity, I was stuck inside and after spending years scratching and kicking the walls, I finally gave up. I laid down with fear in my heart, fear that I'd never escape. But on some level, I think the box was invisible to others. People would talk to me from the outside, they'd even laugh and try to have fun with me, but no one ever tried to step inside with me or help me escape. I'm guessing they didn't know that it even existed. I spent my days gazing from outside my box, looking at everyone enjoying their lives; they seemed happy. They seemed like they'd found some way to live life freely, unapologetically, and without interruption. The more time I spent there, the more my mental health deteriorated.

While no one ever joined me in the box, there were so many things that found their way inside. Familial and societal expectations, directions on how to live my life, insults hurled my way and traumatic experiences all seemed to play on a never-ending loop, swirling through my mind as I sat in the middle of the floor, stoic, but digesting every single thing. Before I knew it, I no longer recognized myself; I could only see whatever version of myself the world had painted of me. As far as I was concerned, this was my

Heaven while also being my Hell. I thought that space was all I would ever know, but, fortunately, I was wrong. It's funny how hitting your face against rock bottom has a way of waking you up. A couple of months before my 24th birthday, after years of standing and sleeping on the cold floor in my box, the only home I'd ever known, I began to fracture from the inside out.

The box and the facade I'd been exuding were beginning to crumble and I couldn't piece it back together again. My smiles became less believable; I had stopped believing the lies I was telling myself and it was clear that something was wrong with me. There was one specific night that still plays so vividly back in my head, almost as if it happened yesterday.

It's hard to realize that four years have passed since this all took place. That night, I remember driving over to an old friend's place, hoping for some kind of solace within myself, some kind of emotional relief. There was always something going on at his house and at that point in my life, I was almost a third roommate, if you judge by the amount of time I spent there. It was always a good place to be. I joined my friend at his house, and two other friends were there. They had been there for a little while before I arrived, so I joined right in or at least I tried to. I slumped onto the couch and my mind began to wander, finding its way to some pretty dark corners. It was almost as if I was in a trance, completely missing the joy that was all around me in that moment.

Do you ever get the inkling or that quiet voice in your mind that tells you that something is wrong, that you should run from whatever circumstance you've found yourself in? I had that feeling, but I couldn't understand why. Here they were, in one room, laughing and joking around, while I found myself in the living room, sitting. Back then, I could not have told you what was happening, but I knew that I couldn't find the courage to fake happiness. That night, something was eating at me, and I found myself sitting alone in a separate room, unable to socialize with them and fake a smile for the one thousandth time in my life. Sitting in that room, a few feet away from friends, I'd never felt more alone. I felt empty, almost as if I had nothing left to give. They continued on with their fun, but after about 15 minutes of ruminating, 15 minutes of being lost in my own mind, I decided to go home. As I walked out to my car, I could feel the storm moving inside me; there was a dark cloud that just wouldn't seem to pass, and it didn't help that it was literally storming that night as well.

My car continued to move towards home, all the way in Lawrenceville, Georgia at that time, but I wasn't in control of it. The car was moving but my mind was somewhere else. I was screaming and crying the entire way home, so much so that I couldn't see the streets or cars around me: everything was a blur. Then I had the thought: "Drive your car off the road" and I sat with that for a while. At that moment, that thought brought me peace. I told myself, "It'll be quick, maybe even painless if you do it right." I wanted it to be over. At 23 years old, I was done. I had lived all the life I thought was worth living and there was nothing anyone could do or say to make me think otherwise. I knew that I wanted to end my life, but I couldn't tell you why. How is it that everything can feel so right and so wrong at the same time? My life was everything I thought it should've been, everything the world told me it should be, but nothing at all like I wanted it to be.

I was in a relationship with a great woman, I was surrounded by friends, my family was happy with me, and I found some stability in my career. I should've been happy, right? But I wasn't. This wasn't the first time I had contemplated suicide, but it was the first time in my adult life and the first time I'd come close to following through with a plan. As great as my life seemed, I knew something wasn't right; something was missing. It wasn't any kind of material possessions, status, or wealth; it was something internal. I was rotting from the inside out and judging by my idea to run my car off the road, something inside me had broken, or at least that's how I felt.

However, in the midst of all of this despair during this drive home, other thoughts began to surface, thoughts of my family. I envisioned my grief-stricken mother, getting the call that they'd found my body. I saw my dad, sitting at home alone, unable to cope with the loss of his son. I saw my aunts, cousins, and grandparents, trying to reconcile my actions and tearfully trying to figure out how to move forward with their lives. These thoughts, though as painful as they were, snapped me out of it. In a way, my family saved my life. I managed to make my way home, spending the rest of the night crying incessantly. I can honestly say I'm not surprised that I reached that level of desperation. After spending my life imprisoned in the cage of other people's expectations of me and what my life should be, I think I was finally losing it.

Growing up in Atlanta, throughout my adolescence and early adulthood, I was the poster boy for conformity. Afterall, my box made sure that I did exactly whatever I was expected to do. Now that some time has passed, I can confirm that I don't even think I was living back then; I was merely existing, serving as a pet and adhering to everyone's commands on how I should live my life. *Take a lesson from me folks: that path will get you nowhere.* In fact, I had the thought to drive my car off the road for a second time months later. I had begun my graduate program and one night after class ended, the same thought came back, "Drive your car off the road." This time, though, my car wouldn't have been veering off into a tree or a pole; it would've been crashing into a median on I-285. It was then that I knew that something in my life had to change; I just didn't know what. My suicidal thoughts were getting clearer, and it wouldn't have been long before I followed through. I didn't know what to do, but I knew damn well that these thoughts wouldn't lead me anywhere productive. Fortunately, starting that graduate program, in the midst of all of that inner turmoil, was one of the best decisions I ever made: it was exactly where I needed to be.

The program pushed me to evaluate my life in every way that mattered, and it couldn't have come at a more perfect time. Just before the program started, I broke up with my girlfriend, I was mourning the loss of two significant friendships, and had all but turned my back on the church, which had been a constant in my life for as long as I've been alive; I had no idea who I was anymore. But if I've learned nothing else, it's that there is beauty in being lost sometimes; you never know what or who you'll stumble across. In losing everything I had ever known, I found everything that I never knew I needed. It was evident that I had a considerable amount of healing and emotional unpacking that needed to be done, which led me to my first therapist later that year. He was a middle-aged white man who specialized in pastoral counseling. Although my belief in the church was waning with each passing moment, I think some part of me chose him as my therapist because I was still holding on to my roots, which were deep in the Christian faith.

Despite my newly discovered aversions to religion, we actually covered a lot of ground. I remember him being warm, accepting, but also surprisingly direct. Our conversations spanned about every area of my life: family, friends, attachment issues, and definitely my control issues.

It didn't take him long to call me out on my need to have control in most spaces in my life and how dysregulated I'd become without it. It's not that everything had to go my way; I simply didn't handle situations where I lacked control well. If I had to examine myself back then, I'd say I was almost robotic in how I lived my life, even with my personality. My life and view of it was similar to always coloring inside the lines; it was inconceivable that life could exist out of the constraints placed upon me. Though others may disagree based on my outward appearance, internally, I always felt cagey, operating within a limited scope.

Truthfully, I wouldn't even say I had a "real" personality prior to beginning therapy. I had compartmentalized so much of myself that I became an extremely watered-down version of whoever I was supposed to be and that wasn't lost on him. He was the first person to step inside my box with me, he sat with me, and I think he may have been the first person I'd come across in life that gave me the license to be myself. The only problem with that? *I had no idea who the hell that was.* When you spend a lifetime playing a character, it's a hard process trying to find your authentic self. My sessions with him were the beginning of a long and excruciating journey. However, in order to begin looking towards a brighter future for myself, we had to explore the sequence of events that led to where I was: me wanting to send my car flying off the highway.

As with most therapists, exploring one's past is undoubtedly always a good place to start. I don't think I had a traumatic childhood by any stretch of the imagination-*or at least that's what I used to think*. Actually, for the first five years of my life, things were actually pretty great. I grew up as an only child, so I received all of my parents' attention. Aside from our road trips and visits to Underground Atlanta, my favorite thing was our family dates, which mostly consisted of us trying out different seafood spots in the city. They would always suggest ordering something for me from the kid's menu, but I was never satisfied until they ordered a plate of crab legs- *just for me*. Even though I needed their help cracking the shells, my crab legs were mine and mine alone.

As I write this now, one could make the argument that I was probably a bit spoiled in the first few years of my life, but I can remember simply adoring my parents. They met in Atlanta some years prior to my conception, but the details on how they actually met will differ depending on which parent you ask. *A couple of decades later and I still don't have a clear consensus so don't hold your breath*. If I had to define my state of being during those first few years, I'd say that it was pure bliss. These are all things that I found myself reminiscing on with my therapist, but of course, at some point we had to get to the nitty gritty and the reasons behind my almost comical dysfunction and cognitive dissonance. I went on to explain to him that while those first few years were everything any child could ask for, things soon took a turn for the worse.

Do you remember what it feels like to lose someone? In life, there are innumerable ways to lose someone, and they each come with their own special brand of pain and mourning. Some people lose loved ones, parts of themselves, due to breakups, murder, prison, terminal illness, suicide, or abandonment, just to name a few. While the ramifications of each loss can differ by circumstances, there is a common trend of brokenness that connects them all. It's a level of brokenness that you wouldn't wish on your worst enemy, a level of despair that brings about every existential question you can think of. Unfortunately, I can relate. I lost my partner in crime and the shoulders that I could always lean on when I was down. I was only five years old when it happened, but I remember that pain and writing this is like reliving it all over again.

I recall feeling like one of my limbs had been cut off and that I was always in danger of bleeding out. Any attempt to repair my wound was futile because the dressing was repeatedly ripped off over and over again, with me never finding a moment of peace, a moment to be free. The once carefree version of myself was long gone and now there was only a glass figurine that could shatter at any moment.

To be completely transparent, I think that on some level, I'm still processing and grieving that loss and it still hurts to talk about. I'm still grieving them, who they were and who *we* were before tragedy ripped us apart. I couldn't have known then, but this was the birthplace of my ensuing depression, anxiety, and, sadly, trauma. In fact, it took me beginning therapy and my graduate program to realize how traumatic that experience was. It shattered my world so much that there are several years from my childhood where I barely have any memories. Honestly, I can remember very little between the ages of five and nine years old. Aside from some vague memories at school and some moments with my family, much of everything else is a blur to me.

Throughout this time, while I presented somewhat normal externally, internally things were changing, and I could feel it; the walls of my box were beginning to form. I became much more fearful of the world around me, but with each passing moment, I also became increasingly anxious about everything. I hated being in new spaces and became anxious around new people. I was always on guard, and I couldn't tell you why. While I didn't know it then, this trauma would reverberate in my life for years to come, completely disrupting my sense of security and fundamentally altering my attachments to everyone around me. To put it plainly, I think that childhood essence and that animated nature died during that time. There was no longer room for creativity, mischief, or individuality; there was only room for survival. It was time for me to grow up, which is exactly what I did. I played my part. I did not disrupt the system, and did whatever was expected of me, even when I didn't want to. I was scared to step out of bounds, so I buried all of my thoughts, emotions and pushed through life somehow.

Believe it or not, I continued on going through life with this mindset for years and society taught me how to cope: suppress, bury, and reject my feelings. So, I did. Without even realizing it, through my socialization at school, home, church, and even sports, I learned that there was a singular way of existing for me, a single way to go through life. In each area of my life, I was being conditioned more and more to not challenge the status quo and to fall in line with everyone else in order to make life "easier." "Man up!" they'd say. So, I did. I buried everything and kept moving along. As my sessions with my therapist continued, we would explore this theme of conformity and coping even more, but it didn't take long for us to shift gears and begin talking about something that I had feared for a while, something that I tried to bury long ago, something that I could always feel bubbling inside of me: my queerness.

In my mind, this was something that I dared not speak about, but I guess therapy would be the appropriate place to discuss it if no place else. While I didn't know it then, my queerness and exploring it would become the nexus of my pain, healing, and prosperity. Up until that point in therapy, I had spent so much of my life denying the existence of my queerness as the culture I was raised in was very much so, "God made Adam and Eve, not Adam and Steve." For a while, that's what

I accepted. I never believed that was the case, but I never spoke out against it either, especially once I started encountering other LGBTQ youth. I'll never forget being in 6th grade and meeting this flamboyant 8th grade boy. While we weren't close, I remember that he was always kind to me in passing, even though the world was so cruel to him. He wore tight clothes; make-up and he was always trying something different with his hair. He stood proud in his femininity and queerness even though it came at a cost: his safety. He was boisterous, queer, black and femme, which wasn't the best combination for a young man living in the Bible Belt.

I don't know what happened to him, but I can still feel the impact that he's had on my life. Unfortunately, I think it is because I witnessed the pain he suffered that I made the conscious decision to fight whatever was rumbling inside me, remaining safely in my comfort zone. I had to fight it because I didn't want to go through life being subjected to the same pain he endured. I was already going through grade school being called a faggot on a daily basis so making myself susceptible to possible physical violence? *I think the fuck not.* In my mind and maybe even those around me, it was imperative that I change myself for the world, not the other way around. Things were already stressful at home, and I knew better than to start ruffling feathers. Interestingly enough, on some level, I think I admired him because he had the temerity to be exactly who he was despite the retribution from students, teachers, and family. At that age, I only ever had one moment where I dared to have a conversation about my queerness with another soul.

After years of daily, verbal bullying from other kids, I finally cracked. At 11 years old, I had begun to tell my mother things that no parent should hear like, “I wish I’d never been born,” and “It’d be easier if I was dead.” When she inquired further, I shut down and refused to speak. Ultimately things reached a breaking point and on a particularly tearful night, on my end, I confessed to her that I’d started to think about guys the way I think about girls, romantically. All I could do was cry because I knew all hell may break loose after making that revelation, but she did the opposite. She held me close and said, “Mama will love you no matter what.” It was exactly what I needed to hear, even if I still believed myself to be the scum of the Earth. In any case, to her credit, my mom realized early on that I needed help processing everything going on within me. She took me to a child psychologist so I could have that outlet, but I refused to speak once I got there. *So, we never went back.* She knew that she didn't have the tools to help me, so she sought out help and I thank her for that, even if I didn't take advantage of the help then.

Throughout the next few years in my adolescence, anytime I saw a guy that was even mildly attractive, I simply wrote it off as, "Oh, he's handsome," but left it at that. I didn't explore it any further and I rejected all advances from guys in the interim. *And let me tell you: the boys were out and ready to play! Ha!* But truthfully, though I did my best to fight it, I'll never forget the moment when I realized that my queerness was something that would never go away. I was 15 years old and there was a guy who rode my bus that I found myself infatuated with. He was two years older than me, quiet, but also seemingly really popular with everyone else. At that age and my level of denial towards my own sexuality, I couldn't conceive that what I was experiencing was a crush. In my mind, I was simply intrigued by him. *Even though there was a moment when he dropped his pencil on the bus and I damn near broke every bone in my body diving to the floor to pick it up for him.* However, I didn't explore it further. Also, let's be clear: *He was straight as a gate.* Nothing would ever have happened between us even if I had the balls to say anything. All I knew was that whenever I saw him in the hallways or on the school bus, I felt joy like never before. It was unlike anything I'd ever experienced.

Of course, he graduated that year and I found myself extremely sad and I didn't know why. "He's just a guy, right? He's not anybody special."

But at that time in my life, he was, and he'll never know it. Years would pass before I experienced anything like that again and I cringe even re-living that particular experience. *I know I'll regret even telling you this at all. *facepalm* Ha-ha!* But it is an experience I'm grateful for because it was a dot in a series of dots that I had to connect in the process of figuring out who I was.

That's actually what therapy allowed me to do: connect all of these dots and begin asking myself those hard questions. "Was I gay and simply in denial? Was I straight and going through the world's longest identity crisis? Or was I bisexual and in denial about that, too?" These were just some of the thoughts. You can imagine how cathartic it was to process all of this with my therapist, but also, being able to process the impact it had on me was a profound moment. My therapist was a hidden gem, and I didn't even realize it at the time. In order to begin exploring these feelings, he encouraged me to branch out and begin exploring the LGBTQ community.

I can't exactly remember how I came across it, but I ended up visiting this church in Atlanta that was led by a gay pastor and his husband. The entire concept was mind blowing to me because I'd never seen anything like it: a church led by two gay men with a congregation that was predominantly LGBTQ. I remember walking into the church and feeling so uncomfortable. The people were some of the nicest and welcoming individuals I'd ever encountered, but the entire scene was a bit of a mind-fuck in a way. Homosexuality and the church had always been mutually exclusive so seeing the two become one was jarring in a sense. I saw lesbian and gay couples walking in with their children. I saw these same sex couples openly showing affection to each other, holding hands here, and a kiss on the cheek there. It was beautiful but confusing for me. My therapist thought that it would be good for me to be able to see healthy examples of queer love and he was right. But, as beautiful as that experience was, it wasn't until some months later where I would begin self-actualizing and accepting who I was.

Sometime after my therapy sessions ended, and months after visiting the church, I was speaking to a close friend, and he was telling me about his plans for the weekend: it was Pride weekend. I had just finished working out when he asked me if I wanted to go out to a couple of gay bars with him. Now, keep in mind that at this time, I was still technically identifying as straight, but my friend was gay. Although we both knew what was going on with me, as I began to peek my head out of the closet, he didn't rush it; he was patient and allowed me to come to him with my truth. He had piqued my curiosity about visiting these bars so even though I was still identifying as straight, I agreed to go with him, and my life hasn't been the same since. That weekend, for the first time in my life, I was surrounded by other queer people, and it was almost a spiritual experience.

From corner to corner, there were transgender women, transgender men, lesbians, and, of course, gay men; I was terrified. It's not that I was scared of everyone there, but it was completely uncharted territory for me. Also, due to my childhood conditioning within the church, I was constantly bombarded with unwanted thoughts like, "Leave or else you're going to Hell. What if you see someone you know, and they tell other people?

God is going to punish you for being here right now!" It didn't help that this was only a year after the *Pulse Nightclub* shooting so I was on edge the entire night, but even so, I knew that I was in the right place, at the right time.

I would continue going out with my friend, visiting different bars, and even started to meet guys, too. It was an interesting time in my life, one that I'm grateful for. But even with this personal growth within myself, in the back of my mind, I knew I'd never feel complete until I started to be honest with my friends and family. At that point, only that one friend knew that I was even thinking about the idea of dating men. It was probably the most nerve-wracking time period in my life, but I started the daunting process of coming out to my friends and family. Throughout that process, though, something surprising happened: I felt a little freer and a little more me every time I told someone the truth about who I am and where I am in life. I found myself calling friends and even seeing them in person and would say, each time, "At this point in my life, I'm open to dating both women and men."

As each conversation took place, my confidence within myself began to increase; my sense of self was getting clearer and clearer. That box that I had lived most of my life in began to dismantle, piece-by-piece. It was an illuminating experience. Honestly, I have to give it to my friends; I don't think I'd be here without them. Most of them showed up for me, held my hand, and never let go-no matter what. It's not lost on me how rare of an experience that can be for a queer person. They stood by me and years later, it still warms my heart. But, of course, that experience wouldn't be complete until I spoke to my parents and the thought crippled me with fear.

There was a lot of processing that needed to be done in that space with my parents and I dreaded it. My mom and I had that one brief exchange when I was a child, but never had any conversations about it further since I continued dating women. Exposing my authentic self would undoubtedly bring so much to the surface, so many conversations that should've happened years ago, but it had to be done. I had spent my life doing everything that was expected of me, being who everyone expected me to be, and I felt that, with this one conversation, all of my hard work of pretending was going to be washed down the drain. I wasn't yet ready to let go of the delusion that I was someone who I wasn't. I felt that their perception of me would change and like many

LGBTQ youth; I thought their love would change, too. I would have rather died than to have that conversation with my parents because I knew where it would go. Now after having had those conversations, I can say that I was only half right.

Their reaction wasn't that of a celebration, but also not exactly the condemnation I was anticipating. When I think of their reactions, one word comes to mind: love. It took some time for me to sit with everything, but now I see that their reactions were rooted in well-intentioned *(but also misguided)* love and a general lack of knowledge of my experience or people who share my life experiences. When you don't personally know any queer people, it's easy to form a depiction of who they are based of societal standards, media depictions, and religious teachings- *and I think that was the case for them.* While they both initially possessed a certain level of disapproval for my sexual orientation, they both were rather fervent in their continual declaration of love as well. To be honest, I think they may have been scared.

I know that my existence puts me at a higher risk of being a victim of a hate crime, which isn't lost on my parents. The church will likely condemn me to Hell and people will utilize my personal life as trivial gossip, which is also something they're especially privy to. There are so many things about my humanity that place a target on my back and that is exactly what they wanted to protect me from. Not only did they have to begin accepting my truth, but they had to begin understanding that conformity would no longer keep me safe and that by walking into some spaces- I was walking into the line of fire. Also, on some level, I imagine that their dreams of how my life would play out likely died when I declared my queerness.

Reflecting back on it, they just needed help understanding and they needed time to process it all and the possible implications, socially, professionally, and existentially. However, with my parents, I've seen that change is possible and we're in a much better place now than when we started. Do I expect them to join me at the next Pride parade? *Absolutely not! Ha-ha!* Do I know that I have their support? I do. However, after all of the conversations I've had with them, I recalled a piece of advice that someone once gave me.

On my first date with a guy, we were speaking about life, the dating scene in Atlanta and coming out to family and friends. He said, "Once you tell your mom and dad, you won't care about what anyone else has to say." That sentence stuck with me and after telling my parents, I found it to be true. *Also, after seeing where things went with him, I can confidently say that this piece of advice was the only good thing to come from that situation.* I'm a firm believer that everyone crosses your path for a reason, even if it's only for a season. He came into my life to impart that piece of wisdom and I'm thankful. After having those hard conversations with my parents, my life changed for the better. My life was far from perfect, but I was finally living my life on my own terms. I became unapologetic in every aspect and refused to continue apologizing for living life in the light. As time went on, and as I continued to be intentional with managing my mental health, I began to see changes within myself.

By this time, my sessions with the therapist had ended. I was too broke to continue the sessions any longer, but because of that start in therapy and being intentional about my growth, I became someone I never thought I could. I became brave, more fearless, and more authentic. All of my existing relationships became stronger, more transparent and I connected easier with new people that I would come across. When I felt, finally, that I didn't have to hide, it seemed like life opened up to me, in a way I thought it never could. The way I started to live was in a way that I thought was only reserved for other people, good people. My life felt like my own and I was no longer going to let the threat of Hell or condemnation from others keep me from continuing to forge my own path. By the time I finished my graduate program, two long years after nearly attempting to drive my car off of the road, I was in a much better head space. For the first time in my life, I wanted to live. But I didn't stop there, I knew that I still had so much work to do within myself. I ended up entering therapy again in order to not only manage my anxiety and depressive episodes, but to learn how to work through them.

I met with a second therapist in 2020 for nearly four months and I'm so thankful for my time with her. She helped me to continue living in my truth, recognize my anxiety triggers, work through my clearly neglected attachment issues and develop an improved sense of self. To anyone who is on the fence about entering therapy services- DO IT! I know that I wouldn't be as healthy in my mind now if I had never explored mental health services. I've seen what happens when we leave our mental health issues unchecked. I've seen people completely unravel from the inside out because they're scared to ask for help. The truth is: We're all going through something: own it!

Sometimes I wonder what my life may have looked like if I'd owned up to my pain sooner, worked through it sooner, and been honest about it sooner. Who would I have been? Who would I be now? What would have happened if I would have been honest about my depression throughout grade school and college? Collectively, I think our power and healing lies in the reality of our pain, which are often shared experiences. None of my experiences that I shared in my story are unique to me. You can probably pull ten random queer people off the street and nine of those stories would likely resemble mine. The only thing that separates us is us.

As I continue navigating the world, with priority to my mental health, I'm cognizant about where I come from and where I'm headed. The young boy who grew up seeing himself as a second-class citizen, the one who used to pray for death, wishing that he'd go to sleep and not wake up; I take him with me everywhere I go, every single day. He serves as a continuous reminder of not only where I've been, but of everything I'm always working on within myself. I don't have it altogether. I don't wake up every morning feeling the best about myself. I haven't reached every dream I thought I would have by now.

Every day is a new beginning and with each passing moment, I'm learning that it is okay not to be okay. I'm continuing to work through my trauma, my attachment issues, spikes in anxiety, and problems with loving myself. I'm learning to let every aspect of myself live out loud, never diluting myself again for others, never allowing any part of myself to hide in the darkness. Every day, I'm learning to accept my imperfections, ask for help when I need it, and to not be ashamed of any part of my journey: Afterall, it's led me to where I am today. Every part of us, even the parts we want to hide, deserve to be seen. You, and all that you are, deserve to live outside of the box and in the sun.

Not So Fun Fact: 44% of Black LGBTQ youth seriously considered suicide in the past 12 months, including 59% of Black transgender and nonbinary youth.

- **55% of Black LGBTQ youth reported symptoms of generalized anxiety disorder in the past two weeks, including 70% of Black transgender and nonbinary youth**
- **63% of Black LGBTQ youth report symptoms of major depressive disorder including 71% of Black transgender and nonbinary youth**
- **Self-harm was reported in 44% of Black LGBTQ youth, including 61% of Black transgender and nonbinary youth**
- **49% of Black LGBTQ youth reported wanting psychological or emotional counseling from a mental health professional in the past 12 months, but not being able to get it.**

-The Trevor Project (2020)

One Bed Left

Kiara's Story

She/Her

I was only seven years old, but I still remember that night so clearly. My sister and I went to this birthday party, and everything was going well until I heard the sound of sirens in the distance. Typically, in Jersey, we would always hear sirens blaring so it usually wasn't anything abnormal, but on this night, the sirens stopped me in my tracks: I completely froze. The night felt off to me; it was something that was different about it, but I couldn't quite put my finger on it. I remember rushing home and realizing how off everything was. When I arrived, I saw that my mom wasn't home, and my grandmother was oddly silent. There was also a family friend over who I didn't care for. I was thinking to myself, "Why is he here?" I remember I kept trying to get my grandmother to say something to me, but she wouldn't say anything. I kept asking her, "What's wrong? What's wrong?!" She turned around from doing the dishes, looked at me and said, "Something happened to your daddy."

When she said it, even though she didn't say he died, chills went over my body, and I knew that he was dead. My first thought after hearing that was, "I think he's dead." I sat on the couch, anxiously awaiting confirmation, and cried. Then we heard the front door. I heard my mom coming up the stairs and I remember hearing moaning, accompanying each step. She walked into the kitchen, sobbing, and said, "He's gone. He's gone." And that was it; It changed my whole life. I would soon learn that my dad had died in a car crash, which was completely bizarre to me. I couldn't quite conceptualize how he was there one day and gone the next. I remember it like it was yesterday. He and my mom were split up at the time and he only lived about two blocks away.

In fact, he lived so close that he would walk to our house, where we stayed with my grandma, to see us every day. This one night, the night he died, he asked to borrow my mom's car to drive home, not that he needed it. He could not have been driving more than 40 MPH, but while he was on his way home, he crashed into a telephone pole and died instantly. That night, the last time I saw him, he pulled me aside and said, "Do you know that I love you?", which was a bit weird to me at the time. It wasn't that my father never told me that he loved me, it was how intentional he was about telling me this specific time. I said, "Yeah, I know." I can remember the way he looked at me, in his eyes, it was almost as if he knew he was going to die that night. But again, everything changed after that.

When I think back to my childhood in Jersey, I'm reminded of so much, including it being the place where I lost my father, but I guess you could say that living in Jersey was a bittersweet experience overall. It was sweet in the sense of it being community driven. Jersey City, at that time, was urban and the crime rate was pretty high, but not on the block I grew up on. Everyone got along with everyone, and kids played in the street, turning on the fire hydrant and playing in the water as it blasted all over the street. At the time, it was pretty similar to the movie *Crooklyn,* kids running all around and surely getting into trouble everywhere we went. Honestly though, I got excited to get up in the morning to go outside and play with my friends. I had so many friends at the time, and we all had grown up together, yelling each other's names up and down the street and riding bikes together, getting into arguments and getting over arguments. It was great in that sense; it was fun.

However, there was a darker side to my time in Jersey, though. Aside from the death of my father, it was the place where I experienced so much trauma in such a short time span. It was the same city where I was physically abused by babysitters while my parents were away. It was the same city where I was repeatedly molested by a neighbor, a teenage boy who I had considered a friend. All of this happened between the ages of four and seven years old. While I can look back on my time there with fond memories, it's impossible to extricate Jersey from the pernicious experiences that plagued my childhood.

The molestation was the first trauma I ever experienced in life. Oddly enough, I didn't know it was as traumatic as it was until I became an adult. I didn't have the words to articulate how I felt and there was no way to know how damaging the experience was to my mental health until I was older. Looking back at some of my behaviors post-molestation, I would say that I was probably dealing with psychosis. At four and five years old, I thought that I was clairvoyant or psychic, but there were moments where I would hear or see things that others couldn't. I can remember a specific moment where I was laying on the edge of the bed one night. My parents were in another room, and I saw what looked like 10 or 12 rats running across the floor and I laid there and stared at the rats walking across the floor. But there were no rats in the house. *At all*. My mom said there weren't any rats in the apartment, but I was convinced that there were.

There was another instance in which I was convinced that I heard bells on the roof so around Christmas time, I thought that I heard a sleigh on the roof as well. But, of course, there was no sleigh and there were no bells. There was even a night where my father slept on a couch in me and my sister's room. I was lying in bed, awake in the middle of the night and I saw a figure of a male standing in the doorway. I thought, "I can see spirits now!" Now, do I believe that there are people who can do those things? Yes, I do believe in the paranormal. But do I believe that's what was going on with me at that time? No, because of what I had experienced.

Looking back as a mental health clinician now, I can see that those were likely brief psychotic experiences due to the trauma. The ramifications of the trauma presented in a myriad of ways and have played out over the course of my life span. Sometime after I was molested, I had vivid dreams about me telling my parents that he had done this to me. To this day, I can still remember the dreams and I was convinced for years that I told my mother what happened to me, and she never did anything. That's how vivid the dreams were. One day, when I was 15 years old while my mother and I were talking, I brought up the molestation like it was nothing because I thought, "She already knows." But she stopped and said, "What are you talking about?" And I said, "I was molested. I told you this happened." Fervently, she continued, "No, you never told me that." I kept stating that I could've sworn I told her and my father. She re-emphasized, “Kiara, if your dad had ever known something like that, he would’ve been in jail. You never told us!” I knew then that it was a lot more traumatic than I thought, but I would also come to realize that there was no processing it with my mom; she would not go on to be a safe haven for me, dealing with this experience.

To be perfectly honest, I didn’t like my mother because she wasn’t there emotionally and some of her words, especially after finding out about the molestation, were toxic. When my mom found out about the molestation, she stated, “Well you must’ve liked it because you kept going back to his house.” *And that was the end of that discussion.* I couldn’t continue talking to her about it because I knew that she wasn’t a safe space for me. We have spoken about it here and there since then, but I knew that in order for me to have a productive conversation with her about it, I needed to get to a more resolved place within myself and heal before I could address it again with someone else. It wasn't her stuff; it was mine.

In my early twenties, it came up again and my mom ended up getting back in touch with someone who lived in the same building as the guy who molested me. She spoke to this former neighbor who was still in touch with the guy who assaulted me and took it upon herself to tell this neighbor what he had done to me. In turn, that neighbor went and told the guy and, of course, he denied it. When that got back to my mom, she came to me and said, "Well he said he didn't do it." I told her, "I don't care what you say or what he says; I remember what happened. I'm not making that up and it's not your place anymore to discuss this with anyone." She responded, "I only brought it up because you're my child," and I replied, "Yes, but I'm not a child. I'm grown."

As time has passed, I would still find myself grappling with the fact that it was someone I knew, a neighbor. It was mind blowing to me, honestly. Thankfully, I was healthy enough in my mind to not have turned against myself, but it triggered my panic system, putting me on guard and putting me on alert, all the time. I spent years not knowing what anxiety was, but I would have to say I was always anxious as a result of it. I always found myself wondering what people's true motives were, thinking the worst of people rather than thinking the best, and it forced me to retreat and spend more time alone because that's when I'm the safest: I can trust myself when I'm by myself.

In addition to genuinely enjoying my own space and finding peace in solitude, it's fair to say that my trauma probably plays a role in why I prefer being by myself, in my own space, now. Without those experiences, I would probably be a bit more social nowadays, a bit more extroverted, but who knows. I think there is a part of my introversion that's a result of this socialization. Now, in learning about myself and prioritizing my mental health, I enjoy that aspect of my personality and I'm aware of where it stems from. As a result of all of this though, I'm stronger, stronger than I ever thought I could be. There's a lot of light, when you're intentional about growth or have a natural resilience about yourself; there's a lot that can come out of pain.

I was intentional about being with me, listening to me, doing my work however I could figure out how to do that. I didn't have the tools and skills to do that along the way, of course, but I was committed to figuring it all out. I got to a point where I would set boundaries, and the only way I would learn how to set boundaries was learning about myself in relationships with other people and that included my mom. I realized, "She's not gonna get it. She won't understand my sexual assault. She's not who I need to talk to achieve any type of healing so we're gonna set this boundary right here: she doesn't get to talk to me about this anymore." Fortunately, I moved on from that and I found that there was so much life that awaited me outside of the trauma in Jersey and within a year after my father's death, we moved out of the state completely.

My father always knew he was going to die young *(he was only 32 years old when he died)* and he always told my mom that when he died, he wanted me and my sister to be raised in Raleigh, North Carolina. My mom honored his request. He passed and within a year, my mom met someone new, and his family lived in North Carolina as well, so we picked up and moved to Raleigh. But the culture change was shocking. I mean, Jersey was racist, but I didn't experience it since everyone I grew up around was brown and white people didn't live in the hood. I didn't experience a lot of that there, but I definitely did when we moved to Raleigh. I went to school and noticed that I was one of two to three black kids in a room of 25 students. I had an accent, and my style was entirely different from everyone else in Raleigh. The style I came with was the way girls dressed up north: the classic Cardi B, the classic Nicki Minaj and Remy Ma. I had gold chains layered, bouffant, silked pressed hair with gold beads in my hair, with a strong northerner accent. I cared about my clothes and fashion. I didn't initially fit in with the black kids and definitely not the southern white kids so there were some difficult transitions at that time, like being called a nigger for the first time in class by a white kid or being bullied by this one black girl *(she was obsessed with me and my clothing)*, and I got into my first fight when I moved to Raleigh, too.

It was tough, but I eventually became friends with some of the girls at school. In addition to dealing with so much at school, during that time my mom also started dating my younger brother's father who was abusive to all of us. There was no peace in the house and by that, I mean that it was always quiet in the house, but there was always this charged, disruptive energy that was around. I never felt settled, never felt secure or safe: not in the house with my mom and my brother's dad and definitely not at school because of how the kids were. As fate would have it, though, a couple of years would pass and my mom would end up putting my brother's father out of the house, when my brother was only two years old. I think, maybe, that's why everything started to come to the surface because I wasn't always on fucking guard all the time- emotionally. All of my trauma, depression, and anxiety finally started to spill out. Looking back at that stage in my life, I would diagnose myself with Major Depressive Disorder (MDD): I was extremely depressed. I stayed in my room a lot. I still socialized, but I was sad and angry all the time. I could not have told you at the time that I was depressed, but I would come home straight from school and lock myself in the room.

However, it was during this time that I found my saving grace, in a way: art. It was art that absolutely saved my life. Hands down. Like if art was a person, I would be worshipping it. Art from childhood to present day has been like peace, it has been safety, it has been freedom, full expression without judgement. I enjoyed music, singing, dancing, and coloring books. I always had notebooks and pens, writing poetry and fictional stories. I was even a sketch artist, sketching whatever came to mind, wherever I would find inspiration. Art was me, I was art. It was the common, calm thread, throughout my existence to this day. It means so much to me. It's that thing that can access me in a way that nothing else can.

Art is spiritual for me, and I was heavy in it from the ages of 15 to 19 years old. I had this yellow radio recorder that had a handle on the end, and I would record myself singing. I would practice that every day. I filled up an entire notebook of poetry, which I think I actually still have. I was drawing and creating all the time, not knowing why. I didn't keep all my art pieces though because I didn't realize how much art meant to me until now. Growing up I thought, "Who's not doing art? Who's not doing this?!" I even minimized my sketching abilities because I was like, "Who can't sketch? People can sketch and put colors together!" I didn't realize at that stage in life that it was truly a gift that I have been given to help me heal. But while I was still working through my own mental health challenges, I came to realize that I had no plans for my future. By the time I was graduating from high school, all of my friends were making plans to go off to college, but I had no interest. *Probably because I was depressed.* I had no desire to go on anyone's campus or share a room with anyone or be around a bunch of people my age so after I graduated high school, I had to enter the workforce, doing little odd jobs here and there.

One day, I was flipping through a magazine, and I saw an ad for massage school. Honestly, I saw the ad, and something in me said, "Hmm," and that made me sit and decide to give it a try. It was a 6-month program and I absolutely loved it. That program took me to places within myself that I never thought I could access. It was one of the most healing experiences of my life. Massage therapy was the first phase of my healing process. It felt different somehow and I saw that I felt different because I cared about how I felt. I cared about who I was, what I wanted, and I was being intentional. That was the difference in myself before massage school and actually starting massage school.

I went into massage school when I was 20 years old and I kid you not, you had to meditate every single day for six months. You would walk into the classroom, the lights were dim, you'd find your seat and you'd sit and continue sitting. I was being taught and had no idea. I got so much out of those mornings and then to learn about the art of massage therapy and learning that it is also a spiritual practice. Everything about what we think and feel gets trapped in the body: everything! So not only was I learning how to feel that in other people, but I was also getting worked on myself. It made me more self-aware and self-reflective, and I connected with myself in a way I never had before. It strengthened my relationship with myself. It was a remarkable experience!

After I graduated massage therapy school, I worked as a massage therapist for a few years, until I got tired of it and realized that it wasn't what I wanted to do for the rest of my life. Looking back, I can see that it was never about becoming a massage therapist, even though I thought it was at that time; it was about the healing that I needed. It's like there was a part of myself that knew better than I knew consciously. It was like, "We gonna heal this thing, girl!" But it took time, and it took a lot of work. Once I finished school and got into the field, I was like "Oh, I don't like this!" I liked the effects of going through the process, though. But I wasn't aware of that when I chose the career. Sometimes, I think people don't know why they're truly drawn to a profession. It could be to access or heal some part of themselves, instead of trying to fulfill some specific goal or aspiration.

In my case, I got what I needed from that experience and then I moved on. At 24 years old, after I left behind my career as a massage therapist, I went to Hawaii to work on a cruise ship for about five months as a waitress. I don't think I had any specific career aspirations in mind when I decided to go, but I knew that something had to change. I needed something different and while I didn't know it when I made the decision to work on the cruise ship; my life would, indeed, never be the same after working there. I met my ex-boyfriend, Mark, on that ship and to say our worlds collided would be an understatement.

Before you work on a cruise ship, you have to train. They sent me to this seaman school in Maryland and at the time, the school was designated for training for military seamen and Mark was a part of that training cohort, though he wasn't a part of the military. He was on one side of the school training, while I was on the other side for the training of the crew members. He was serving food and I was walking through the line to get food and that's where we saw each other for the first time, which was sometime in February of 2007.

In August of that same year, we were assigned to the same cruise ship, with him continuing his training while I began working on the ship. One day, I was sitting in the cafeteria and in walked Mark. I didn't know anyone else on the ship, but I remembered when I saw him, "That's the guy from the school. We locked eyes in that food line." *And it was all downhill from there*. But again, I believe wounds are attracted to wounds. There was no reason for me to engage with him. Did I find him super attractive? No, he looked like a lot of the other guys on the ship. Why him? Unhealed trauma probably. I remember he was sitting down eating his cereal and I walked over, and I sat next to him and said, “Hey! You want to have a conversation?” or something like that. We ended up talking all night, and the next day and the next day and it kept going. To this day, I cannot tell you what attracted me to him.

We continued talking and eventually decided to start dating officially. After working on the cruise ship for a while, I ended up moving to Charlotte, North Carolina with Mark, which was the compromise we agreed on. We both wanted to move to Atlanta, but my massage therapist license was in North Carolina. I hadn’t decided to go back into massage therapy as a career, but I had to work and pay bills until I decided my next career move. I had to wait to get a Georgia license, so we agreed to meet in the middle. We decided to wait, save some money and after a year, we finally moved to Atlanta.

The next 10 years of my life were a rollercoaster. I was still working as a massage therapist at the time of our move when I had the thought to go back to school. I completed undergrad and grad school all while being in this relationship, attending the University of Phoenix for undergrad and Messiah University for graduate school, majoring in psychology. My entire education was completed virtually. I can't even tell you why I decided to pursue psychology except for maybe to heal myself. Therapy was a part of my graduate program, with us having to undergo six sessions. *It was either that or take some kind of personality profile test.* It was cool and a nice introduction to therapy, which I was grateful to have especially during that time in my life. The longer that Mark and

I stayed together, the more I saw him for who he truly was, and I can't say that I liked what I saw. While he never physically struck me, he was abusive in every other way. He never failed to find a way to beat me down verbally and mentally. He was as charismatic as he was manipulative and cheating wasn't the worst that he had to offer. The final straw that led me to eventually leave the relationship wasn't in a way I could've ever imagined.

He had said a lot of dangerous, hurtful, and unacceptable things over the 10 years, but on one particular night he threatened me, physically threatened me. He used the word "violence." Something in me clicked that night, somewhat, and it brought about my awareness of his awareness. Even though I knew that he knew what he was doing, emotional abuse is never explicitly harmful, it's subtle. He had made clear threats over the course of the relationship. You may ask, "Why did she excuse that?" Simply put, I was invested in the relationship. But this night, the potential harm was so explicit, more explicit, and visceral than ever before. It was always implicit prior to, like he would allude to it, but this night was different. He actually said, "Don't make me get violent with you." He had never made a statement that direct to me while holding a weapon. He was standing in front of me, holding a broken glass bottle, and in that moment, I was in my head having a conversation with myself. There was a part of me, in my mind, that turned around and looked at myself and said, "What we bout to do about this? We've excused way too much. Why? Don't know. We still need to figure some shit out, but this is clear! I'm actually in danger!"

That's what I was saying to myself. It was clear as to what he was capable of and what he could do. It was so unacceptable. This was the moment when things had to escalate; I could no longer look away from the problem. I didn't have any more rope and he didn't either. I had the realization that I could die "accidentally." That all flashed in my mind at that moment. Ironically enough, he left for a vacation that night and I didn't get any sleep, staying up all night crying because I knew what I had to do. For confirmation, I called a domestic violence abuse hotline. I asked them, "Is what I'm going through abuse?" The lady on the other end said, "Yes. Honey, you're being and have been abused. What would you like to do?" She said, "Just so you know, there aren't any more beds in any of the other shelters, but we have one bed left here. It's yours if you want it."

I don't know, it was like in massage school, that part of me that's always wise and knowing said, "Go!" So, while he was gone on vacation, I packed up all my stuff and I was gone before he came back. I even texted him, telling him that I was leaving, and I ended up staying in the shelter for six weeks. Looking back, I texted him because I was afraid of him; I was scared of him. I'm so excited for whoever is going to read this and relate to this story because it's such a confusing and warped experience, to go through abuse, especially emotional abuse. Understand that in no way, shape or form am I trying to minimize any other form of abuse, of course, but physical abuse is clearer and tangible. Emotional and psychological abuse is damaging, in that it is not as tangible, it's sneaky and can often go overlooked; even the strongest minds can be drawn in. I was so afraid of him and, equally, so in love with him. Now I understand why, especially after becoming a clinician. I left and went to a shelter that night.

While he couldn't find me after he got back from vacation, due to being at a safe house, we still talked via text. To any woman who has experienced abuse, listen: most women go back at least seven times. Why? Because you are bonded to the person you've been in a relationship with. Also, it's worth noting that abuse is not occurring 100% of the time, despite what some people may think. It was loving *(tons of love bombing)* and there's a lot of hyping you up. The abuser knows and, unbeknownst to them sometimes, feed those parts of you that need to be healed. This year, I was able to piece together how I ended up in that situation with Mark or that relationship at all: it all goes back to my dad. I was so young when he died and I've spent most of my life canonizing him, but completely disregarding the reality of who he was. I love my dad and I always will, but it took me some time to be completely honest with myself about who he was.

He was physically abusive to me and my sister, but he always told us that he loved us. That is where I made the connection between love and pain and I can see how I was able to always forgive Mark; it's what I was used to, it wasn't abnormal to me in the least bit. While I can recognize that my father loved me, I have also begun to realize the long-term impact of his actions. However, I've been fortunate enough to take advantage of therapy and other mental health services, which have profoundly impacted my healing journey. I was even able to take advantage of therapy while in the safe house, with us having to meet with the director once a month. The director was like this yogi, bald, black woman with soothing music playing in her office, with this being my first time back in therapy since I was in grad school. After I left the shelter, I packed up my car and moved back in with my mom in Raleigh. I went into the shelter in August 2017 then moved home in October of 2017 and spent the rest of the year there with my family. Now, being four years removed; I can see how difficult of an experience that was. Even after officially breaking up, we didn't officially cut ties. We still talked, met up, had dinner, and connected. I think another misconception surrounding leaving abusive relationships is that once your physical body is removed from the situation, your heart and mind are removed too. That's simply not true.

If people could put into perspective the amount of time I was in an emotionally abusive relationship, and the amount of time it would take to rewire my brain, to untether myself completely from him; It's heart-breaking. I cried a lot in the shelter and felt like a complete fool for being in the shelter for six weeks and then talking to him again. It was like, "What was the point of the shelter?!" These were all the judgements I had about myself, which was a part of my healing process. What made the difference is that I was able to be that honest with myself and then be my friend and say, "Wait a second. Why do you feel this way? I get that you want to judge yourself about it, but be realistic about it, too: this was painful. You were in a committed and bonded relationship with someone." I had to move out of the emotional space and move into that intellectual space, so I started to research, "Why do people stay with their abusers?" and "trauma's impact on the brain and what you're drawn to." So, from four years old to when I ended things with Mark, a lot of things had happened in my life. My outlook on life had been completely shaped by a myriad of traumatic experiences.

I sometimes think about what type of glasses I must've been wearing this whole time throughout my life. After Mark, I had to learn to take those off. Those glasses that I was wearing were being formed and fitted to my face by every experience I had growing up. The molestation formed a part of those glasses, my dad's death, my mom's abusive relationship, my relationship with Mark; everything was being seen through the same lens. I was going through life wearing these glasses that are fitted to my face, the lenses are smudged, and I can only see life this one way for the longest time. The glasses were a part of my identity, so it took a lot of work to clean the glasses, wipe all the smudge off and rewire my brain. It takes a lot to do that and I'm still working on it, setting boundaries with people, working on self-care and being intentional every day. I'm checking in with people I trust and talk about what I'm thinking, not for validation but for clarity to make sure I'm seeing things healthily. Healthiness, in every way- especially mentally and emotionally, is what I'm looking forward to from here on. Therapy has been a big part of this journey as well, with me also entering therapy again in 2019, completing about 6-8 sessions. Those sessions were extremely helpful so I'm pretty grateful for the experience.

Overall, I want continued inner peace from now on. I don't know if there's anything external that I want; it's all internal because that's where true happiness resides *(Where the money resides, where the money resides! Ha)!* That's all I want for myself moving forward; I have me. My goal is to continue building my glow internally and allow it to show up outwardly. Not doing what feeds my ego, but what feels my soul. Soul food all day. That means being careful about choosing who I am going to be in relationships with on every level, having healthy boundaries, and dedicating my life to art- to what has been my confidant, my best friend, and what saved my life. I've forgiven all the trauma and those that have caused it and I'm learning how to move forward from it all every day. I can forgive a lot of what has happened and not really have an emotional attachment to it. There's still some healing to do, but I think healing transforms to growth; we're always growing. I'm still becoming.

Not So Fun Fact: More than 40% of Black women will experience domestic violence in their lifetime, according to the Institute of Women's Policy Research's Status of Black Women in the United States. In comparison, 31.5% of all women will experience domestic violence. A report from the National Center for Victims of Crime found that 53.8% of Black women had experienced psychological abuse, while 41.2% of Black women had experienced physical abuse.
More disturbingly, Black women are 2.5 times more likely to be murdered by men than white women. In the overwhelming majority of these cases — 92% — the person who killed them knew their victim. 56% of these homicides were committed by a current or former intimate partner. Nearly all —92% — of these killings were intra-racial, which means that they were committed by a Black man against a Black woman.

-The Blackburn Center (2020)

We Are Humans First

Jeremiah's Story

He/Him

It was a Sunday, sometime in October of 2020 and I can remember the day so clearly. It was another sunny day in California, but while everything was bright and sunny on the outside, I felt like I was dying on the inside. I was standing in a graveyard, with a bottle of whiskey and a baggie full of my drug of choice. Standing out there, hours passed, with me drinking, getting high and crying non-stop. There was so much that led me to that moment. There were years of pain and trauma that led me to this breaking point. No matter how much I cried or tried to numb myself with the booze or the drug; nothing could take it all away. As this moment was one of my lowest points, it was also a new beginning in several ways.

If anything, I would say that this moment in the graveyard was a culmination of experiences and pain, finally colliding. At that moment, I didn't know what to do, where to go or who to turn to for help, but I knew I needed it. Up until then, I had continued doing my best to push through everything life had thrown at me, but I was officially at a place where I began contemplating taking my own life, which is something I haven't shared with many people. To be honest, it was beginning to look like a more probable end to my story because I was tired, tired of fighting every day or trying to manage all of the thoughts and feelings swirling in my head. But like a lot of people, my story didn't start this way. Actually, I have some pretty fond memories to look back on.

I was born and raised in the Bay area in California. My parents met in New York City, with my dad being African American and my mom being a Filipino woman. My dad was working in finance at the time and pretty soon, they welcomed my older brother into the world. Shortly after he was born, they chose to relocate to the Bay area, which is when I arrived. We bounced around a bit from house to house due to my dad having a lot of different jobs, with us even moving to Hawaii for four years. My dad lived out there when he was a teenager, fell in love with it so he moved us all there for a while and we had an amazing time.

Life was good, to be honest. We spent every day at the beach, walking along the docks and the creeks, visiting parks and malls; it was like being on vacation all the time! Most importantly - it was my dad's happy place. I didn't know how much he loved that place, and I can see how moving back to the Bay area was probably a sad time for him. But I'm glad that I have those memories to look back on because there was no way for us to anticipate what would happen next. I'm not sure there is anything that could've prepared us, but maybe that's just how life goes. We moved back from Hawaii to the Bay area in 1998, and within a few months, on December 18th, 1998, my father committed suicide. He bought a gun a week before Thanksgiving and shot himself in the head a week before Christmas. He killed himself during an office Christmas party in Santa Clara. The entire ordeal threw our family for a loop, for sure. I knew that my family had a bit of history with depression, addiction, and suicide, but there was no way for us to know that this would happen.

Honestly, it was a trip, dealing with my dad's death. Yesterday, my old boss told me that his daughter got accepted to UCLA, which is great news for her. While she's busy celebrating her great news, her best friend is grieving due to finding out that her dad killed himself. He was a single father, raising her after her mom bounced on them, but it got me thinking: what's the best out of a bad situation? Was I lucky that I was a kid when my dad killed himself, since I was a bit aloof at the time? Or would I have handled it better or worse if I were an adult when it happened? If I were 18 years old and going through a lot of hormonal changes, would I have responded better or worse? It's tough living in that space: the survivors of suicide. I found myself joining many support groups to heal, in addition to group therapy, which really helped over the years. But, in the beginning, I was against bringing any kind of attention to his death at all. I didn't want to address it.

I used to lie when people asked how my dad died. I would say he got into a car accident, or someone murdered him; anything other than he killed himself. I remember how my mom would drag me to therapy offices after my dad died and I was so embarrassed, so much so that I didn't want to even get out of the car. It makes me think about the stigma around mental health and suicide. As a kid, having no baseline knowledge of suicide or anything like that, I was embarrassed to tell people that my dad killed himself because of what they might think of me. You know, I was the kid whose dad committed suicide, "What are people gonna think?" The stigma around it is immense. I can remember sitting in the waiting room at the hospital in the therapy department at 14 years old, wondering who else would be there and hoping I didn't see anyone I knew. After all, I was there to see a shrink; it was rough, and I think it led to some bad patterns. However, I wasn't the only one struggling with all of this, as my brother took my dad's death pretty hard, maybe even harder than I did at the time. I'd even go as far as to say that our dad's death broke my brother beyond repair.

When he went off to college, my brother struggled with abusing both alcohol and drugs, so much so that he's now on Supplemental Security Income (SSI) for disability as a result of the extensive alcohol and drug usage. Due to all of this, I'm my brother's primary caregiver now. My brother, and I are less than two years apart and we were always close growing up, but we took two different paths after my dad's death. As he went to college, he suffered from depression and addiction, and I think he used alcohol and drugs to mask his pain. Maybe it's because I was younger at the time of my dad's passing, *(I was almost 10 years old at the time and my brother was just shy of 12 years old)*, but it affected him way differently, much earlier, while I feel like I didn't feel the impact of it until years later.

Luckily, my mom managed to pull through and raised us after my dad's death. She was an elementary school teacher and eventually opened up a nursing home here in the Bay area, running her own small business for a while. Fast forward, my mother tried to put my brother through college, and she definitely put me through college, working and managing her own business at the same time. While I was in college my senior year, my mother received a cancer diagnosis and I was terrified of what might happen next, especially after my dad's death some years earlier, but she beat it and it was a great time for sure. She even made it past her five-year mark, which signifies that you are cancer free. That was a beautiful moment and I'm glad that we were able to share it.

After she was diagnosed with cancer, I helped her shave her head and at her five-year anniversary of being cancer free, I had her shave my head; I wanted to stand in solidarity with her. It's something we were able to smile about. But in the 6th year, the cancer came back and within two months, she was gone. It was a surreal experience. I mean, this woman taught me more than I learned in college, and I tell everybody that, including people in interviews. She taught me how to navigate life, how to run a business; she was motivating. She was in a coma for a few days due to the medication, but right before she passed away, the moment before she passed, she opened her eyes, looked up at me, took her last breath, closed her eyes, and died. It was 5:25 am, October 3rd, 2018. It goes without saying that seeing that really messed with me.

For a second there, I thought I was making it up when I told people this story because it was just bizarre. Sometimes, I sit back and look back on the two months I spent in the hospital with her; it was me and her. One day, while still in the hospital, she told me, “Please don’t bring your brother. Don’t let him watch me die. He can’t handle it.” I’m glad it was me and not my brother because he probably wouldn’t have been able to handle it; he was fragile. But at the same time, I don’t know if I was able to handle it because in the coming months after her death, I quit my job and I took a much-needed break from everything.

There were many reasons why I left my job as a recruiting manager, but the biggest one was because I watched my mother take her last breath. The trauma from my dad's death, combined with the trauma from my mom's death messed with me. I think that I didn't fully feel the gravity of my dad's death until after my mom's death, with everything coming to a head at one time. My whole support system used to be my mom, which is why my whole world fell apart when she died. Trying to figure out how to navigate life without her there by my side was heartbreaking. Throughout everything, even my dad's death, she was the one constant thing, the person I could go to for help, guidance, and support. After my mother's death and quitting my full-time job, I eventually started working at a plant store for minimum wage and I didn't even care. I needed a break from life, but with the Coronavirus pandemic going on, things kind of began spiraling out of control. I was so depressed, very depressed and in an effort to try to help myself, I utilized different therapeutic techniques like emotional flashcards and EMDR therapy, but I don't think it worked.

At some point, I began finding comfort in a particular drug of choice to begin coping; it was a bit like a security blanket, but I became addicted to it. It's kinda crazy to think back to last year and to realize that I was a full-time drug addict for the better part of the year. Every moment from when I woke up to when I went to sleep, if I slept, I was using drugs. Not only did I quit a good job as a recruiting manager at a startup company in the midst of all of this, but I also spent all of my savings on drugs, tens of thousands of dollars; I was so lost, man. Somehow, though, even through this pandemic and my drug use, I started my own business: a plant company.

I took everything I knew from working at the plant shop and used that knowledge to build my own business. With everything going on in my personal life *(and especially with the COVID pandemic raging on)*, I felt like my back was against the wall, but I knew that it was now or never. I saw a quote online a few months prior, while I was still doing research on the business: "Do it now, because sometimes, later becomes never." I was sold! After reading that, I was motivated, and I knew that it was time to get out of my comfort zone and get down to business. Yes, I was still using drugs heavily, but I was hustling seven days a week for the business *(the drugs slowed me down, so I had to work 50% harder to keep up)*. I had to get the best plants, do marketing, take product pictures, interact with customers, build my brand, and create partnership opportunities. I knew that this was the right avenue for me, especially given the cause that I was working to support: mental health awareness.

I've always had this theme in my life of working at mission driven companies like companies in health tech or education tech, *(which was inspired by my mother since she worked in education).* Also, suicide prevention has always been a thing for me because of my father. Specifically, suicide prevention within the black community is a pretty big focus of mine; it's stigmatized and not talked about at all, definitely not in any kind of meaningful way. The conversation surrounding suicide prevention in black communities is not where it needs to be, in reference to the resources or lack thereof. They're not commercialized, so to speak. So when I started my business, I knew that I didn't want to only sell plants for the sake of selling plants: I wanted to do more with it. People out here in the Bay sell plants for crazy prices, crazy markups and they're putting the money in their pockets. I understand that everyone has to pay their bills and what not, but as an entrepreneur, I feel that there is a duty and a calling to give back to the community. You know, across the street from me is public housing, I want to give back to the people that live there, the people in my neighborhood.

With my business, I was able to partner with a local non-profit that provides crisis intervention services to those that need it, 24/7. Every month, a portion of my plant sales go directly to their volunteer organization so they can prevent crises. Text and call-line volunteers are there; it's a county wide thing. That's how I try to give back. But still, it's funny because as I was building the business, I was highly addicted to a particular drug, and I was trying to make things work. I had a great job, so I bought a house and had my partner, Rachel, and several roommates living with me. Without the support of my partner, I definitely would've lost it all.

By October of 2020, two years after my mom's passing, I was still struggling. After finding myself standing in the graveyard, drinking, crying, and getting high, I decided to call a rehab center and checked myself in. I was like, "This is not normal. My behavior isn't normal." I would go down various denial patterns and say, "Well I have a friend that drinks every day, too, so it's not that bad." Or, "I have friends that do way worse drugs than I do. They have the problem, not me." But as I started thinking about my habits over the past year and when and where I chose to do drugs and the things I did, I knew I had to make a change. I blacked out at my girlfriend's birthday party after I had sworn that I threw my stash away. My girlfriend caught me, high and clearly out of my mind. I would hallucinate about killing myself and there were a few times I had to have my girlfriend call my job and tell them, "Jeremiah's not feeling good." Rehab was my only solution, as other options hadn't worked.

After my mom's death, I sought out group therapy for grief, one-on-one individual therapy, and even psychiatry, so I could get help with anti-anxiety and anti-depression medications. I tried everything. I even tried getting services from this one particular healthcare system, that's pretty big. Maybe they were understaffed, but it took six weeks to get an appointment and if you had a cancellation or if anything went wrong in the system, you would not see your therapist for months. I think the average time for seeing a therapist was maybe once a month for 30 minutes. My thought process was, "What am I going to talk to you about once a month for 30 minutes? I'll have to keep getting to know you all over again." It was a pretty painful experience, so I started seeking out public options, like the rehab program I ended up going into.

The rehab program was state funded and that's when my eyes were opened to the support they offer. I mean, they tailored a whole recovery plan to you. They had 2-3 counselors working with me, checking in and rooting for me. They made me promise to stay clean, work out, look for work, and most importantly, reflect on how my drug use had flipped my life upside down. As addicts, we were all in denial at some point or another, but the rehab counselors helped us realize that we were the only ones to blame, and it was time to rethink our views of the world and what got us to this point. Also, what I've discovered is that there are so many misconceptions about addicts out there in society. People who suffer from addiction are not bad people; their cards are dealt a certain way, different from what some other people might understand. For starters, people typically describe addicts as just that: addicts. The rehab clinic tried to help us change that mindset and show us that we are just regular people who *happen to suffer from addiction*, like how I suffer from allergies, or my brother suffers from depression: we are more than the ailments we struggle with.

People need to remember that we are humans before we are addicts; we are HUMANS first. Keeping that in mind helps us to normalize the pain of those that suffer from addiction and helps to destigmatize it altogether! I think people should know that not every person who suffers from addiction is going to steal your bike or swipe your wallet for cash. Most of us want to be left alone and we feel like if we're only hurting ourselves, then there's nothing wrong with this behavior. It's a terrible way to think, but it's true, at least for me. It's a terrible way to think because by hurting ourselves, we're inevitably hurting those we love. Think about it: my dad thought he was simply ending his own misery, but by committing suicide, he inevitably shattered a whole entire family system and shattered people, like my brother, for a lifetime. Fortunately, though, just as there are people who judge those that suffer from addiction, there are those who are committed to being a friend whenever you're in need.

As I started rehab and started to get clean, two weeks passed and an old coworker and friend, Sarah, called me. She said, "I'm at this new company now and I know you've been battling with mental health recently, but we're looking to do some hiring. Could you come help us for a few weeks as a contract employee?" I was a bit hesitant, but replied, *"Um...yeeessss?"* I didn't know if I was ready to go back to full time recruiting. I was doing it part-time, but I was also working at the plant store, trying to build my business, but I also had to tell her, "Sarah, I go to rehab every day for drug abuse. I don't know. As the head of HR, I know this will make or break me getting the job, but is that okay?" That month, I began the job, working as a full-time recruiter. As of today, Sarah is one of a handful of people who I've shared my story with. She has had my back this whole time, helping me through that entire time period in my life; she really did a lot for me.

My life changed that month, in the best way possible. After checking myself into rehab, I landed this new job, moved out of an area that was close to my drug dealer and began focusing on the business and giving more money each month to the non-profit that I support for suicide awareness. But I've learned that catching is not the same as keeping; I have to maintain. There was one point when I had $400 in my business account, but I made a commitment to give $500 to the crisis support service. My motivation was helping others, so I wasn't thinking about running a sustainable business. I was literally about to go into debt and transfer the money when my girlfriend came and sat down next to me. She asked how much was in the account and how much I was donating. She pointed out, “You realize that if you don’t help yourself, then you can’t help other people?” That was a lesson for me and one I would have to take with me as I begin working towards my goals for the business.

One of the goals is to begin impacting policy in reference to mental health. We, me and Rachel, are always talking about helping to advocate for policies that will help people in crisis. We talk about the idea of defunding the police and the overall idea of reallocating public funds in order to fund mental health efforts and awareness. After going through publicly funded programs for rehab, I see the value there and want to help bolster that and if I can do that through selling plants and initiating advocacy with local politicians and organizers, then that’s what I'm going to do. I love recruiting for a mental health company because I get to support mental health causes in my day job and in my business so it's motivating for me, but I know I won't retire being a recruiter; I'll retire selling plants and supporting mental health as the CEO of my company. Looking at my own story, I know this is a cause worth advocating for.

Given some of my addictive tendencies over the past year, I don't think I've been grounded or a good person. In fact, I've probably been terrible in many ways through this grief and addiction process, but I know that I have to keep going, keep working on myself and working towards the causes that are important to me. I haven't taken a lot of time off from work in the past four or five months; I think that's what keeps me going. Aside from Christmas and Thanksgiving, every day has been dedicated to promoting suicide awareness, but it honestly doesn't feel like work. I care about mental health for black and brown communities; that's where my focus is. Other communities (*white communities*) write the books on these things, and they have the funding. I heard a story on the radio the other day, in Silicon Valley, there were some all-white charter schools in wealthy neighborhoods that got a secret dose of COVID vaccinations, and I'm not surprised; that's what privilege gets you. So, in my mind, I began wondering about exactly how we can do something at the state level to fund programs for people that look like us? I don't admire my childhood at all, and I want to make sure that no one has to go through the same thing I went through with my dad. I wish I had both of my parents here, to be completely frank with you. But I don't and there's no changing that.

When talking about my dad, my grandma used to say, "He was a provider. He manned up and he dealt with life as it came." But in my mind, I think, "Look at where that got him." So, although I have a mortgage to pay, my brother to support, and people that depend on me, I'm trying to find balance in my daily life because I don't want to end up like him. He was only 42 years old when he died: I'm 33 years old now. Fortunately, I have a pretty great support system that helps keep me on track. My girlfriend is my rock and my aunt, my dad's sister, reminds me of where I come from: she's a constant reminder of my roots. Keeping in touch with folks, in general, helps to keep me going.

With my business, I like to share a little bit of what I love with people, like when we throw pop up events on weekends, we have a bubble machine, R&B music playing, lights, plants, and maybe even some dog treats. *We don't have a dog, but we bring treats for other people's dogs.* In a way, these are all little pieces of me that I'm able to share with others; it reminds me of who I am and what I'm working towards. I think that it's important to keep your mind healthy and be motivated by staying true to who you are. I was so stressed and depressed last year. I was suicidal and I was on drugs, and I almost went to electroshock therapy because I didn't know where else to turn. When I think about all of those times, when I was really stressed out, I see that they were times when I felt like I was selling out or not doing what I was supposed to be doing. So having a path for yourself and sticking to it, staying honest to your true nature and a constant reminder that as long as you're putting good out there, you are enough. Never let anyone tell you that you aren't worthy or that you don't deserve better. There can be times in relationships or at work where things aren't working out, but remind yourself of everything you've done to get this far and know that you're pretty fucking amazing.

Not So Fun Fact: While addiction is a medical disease, it remains a stigmatized disease, which affects substance dependence research, prevention, treatment services and legal policy in the United States... Members of racial and ethnic minority groups are most likely to experience barriers that impede their ability to access substance abuse treatment. We must re-examine how to best make accessible, retain, engage, and support African-Americans individuals who are seeking to end their substance dependency.

-American Psychological Association (2017)

Acknowledgements

The process of writing this book has been illuminating to say the least. While all of the participants, Olivia, Derrick, Lydia, River, Kiara, and Jeremiah all come from different backgrounds and have different stories, there are so many commonalities between all of them. Being able to look at the intersection of grief, trauma, depression, substance abuse, anxiety, and suicidality between the six of them has been illuminating, but also extremely saddening at the same time. Their origin stories are all different, but the pain has been eerily similar in several ways; that's something that I had to sit with for a moment because I was absolutely in awe. Through socialization, we've learned to hide so much of ourselves and so much of our story, but in this process, it has been further cemented in my mind that we are not all that different from one another. In fact, I see myself in all of their stories and I think others will, too.

When I embarked on this journey, I didn't know which way things would go, but I'm elated with the end result. I want to thank everyone that made this book possible.

River- you are greater than every struggle you've faced and I'm so glad that you're still here, inspiring others with your story. You are more powerful than you realize; never forget that.

Lydia- your honesty, and transparency blew me away and I could not be prouder to have you take part. You are a shining light and I truly believe that the world would be better off with more people like you.

Derrick- the bravery that you exemplified not only in telling your story, but also throughout your life is so admirable. Your strength and resilience are breathtaking. Please, never change.

Olivia- you told your story with such fluidity and confidence, and I know you will be an inspiration to many. Your story may not have started off the way you would have wanted, but I know the journey and ending will be nothing short of beautiful.

Jeremiah- you are an example of everything that I've always strived to be: determined, transparent, honest, and sincere. There is no doubt in my mind that your parents are beyond proud of who you've come to be.

Kiara- I am endlessly in awe of you; your heart and your commitment to bettering yourself is so heartwarming to witness. You are literally a national treasure and I feel blessed that God saw fit for us to cross paths.

Also, I have to take a moment to acknowledge my team who helped me bring this dream to life. To Kerris, Joshua, and Brianna, my test readers, and partners in life- thank you! Thank you for taking the time to go through these stories with me, giving your honest feedback and helping me make sure that this book would be the best it could be. I love and appreciate you all more than words can describe.

Anna- my friend and one of the greatest artists I've had the pleasure to know, thank you for all that you've done and your patience with me. I told you about my vision for the artwork for the book and you brought it to life with such ease and precision. You continue to amaze me and I'm so grateful for you. I know that this is only the beginning for you!

MC- you were a lifesaver throughout this process, especially when it came to actually preparing to register and distribute the book. (My anxiety was on TEN getting through this part of the process. Ha!) Thank you! Thank you! I couldn't have done it without you.

Tamika- my wonderful editor, you did the damn thing! Thank you so much for taking the time, going page by page, helping me to get this book and these stories in tip top shape. You were a joy to work with and I look forward to being able to work with you again. In fact, it's been an absolute dream to work with each and every one you.

Additionally, I think the most beautiful part of writing this book and telling these stories has been witnessing how far one can go when they are intentional about their mental well-being. I've been able to see, with my own eyes, everyone find freedom outside of the constraints that life has placed on them. Whether they were trapped by substance abuse, grief, or even trauma, they made their way to freedom. They are always on the path to not only improving their mental health, but also maintaining it. They have all certainly made progress from where they started. I think that is absolutely something to smile about, something to celebrate.

Lastly, to the reader, thank you for even taking the time to read this book of mine. I hope you've found it to be helpful in some way and that maybe you've been able to get some insight into beginning to confront your own problems. I may not be there to help you in person but know that I'm always with you in spirit.

List of Resources

National Suicide Prevention Lifeline is a 24/7, 365 days a year service, offering crisis intervention and suicide prevention services as needed. If you or anyone you know find yourselves thinking about suicide or harming yourself, please call 1-800-273-8255.

National Domestic Violence Hotline is a 24/7, 365 days a year service, offering support to survivors of domestic violence. Trained advocates are there to offer free and confidential services during crisis, along with offering education and referrals as well. They can be reached at 1-800-799-7233 or text "START" to 88788

Substance Abuse and Mental Health Services Administration (SAMHSA) is a free and confidential hotline aimed at providing treatment referral/ information to individuals and families facing mental and/or substance use disorders. They can be reached at 1-800-662-HELP (4357), 24/7, 365 days a year.

Therapy for Black Girls is an online platform, advocating for the overall mental wellness of Black women and girls. The platform can help get you in touch with mental health clinicians in your area, while also providing helpful psychoeducation through their blog and podcast. Any general inquiries can be emailed to info@therapyforblackgirls.com.

Therapy for Black Men is an organization that is dedicated to breaking the stigma of mental health and provides culturally competent care to black men. They have a stacked directory of both therapists and coaches that are waiting to help, if you're ready. They can be reached at (646) 780-8278 or info@therapyforblackmen.org.

About the Author

Corey Harper is a mental health professional, born and raised in Atlanta, Georgia. Throughout his professional career, he's worked in multiple roles at a psychiatric stabilization facility, and served as a therapist for children and adults with a history of sexual trauma. He earned his Bachelor of Science degree, with a focus in Sociology from Kennesaw State University. He went on to obtain a Master of Science degree in Clinical Counseling Psychology.

Sources

(n.d.). Retrieved from https://www.parkview.com/community/dashboard/black-men-and-suicide-breaking-the-stigma

All Black Lives Matter: Mental Health of Black LGBTQ Youth. (2020, October 05). Retrieved from https://www.thetrevorproject.org/2020/10/06/all-black-lives-matter-mental-health-of-black-lgbtq-youth/

Black women, the forgotten survivors of sexual assault. (n.d.). Retrieved from https://www.apa.org/pi/about/newsletter/2020/02/black-women-sexual-assault

Center, B. (2020, February 26). Black Women & Domestic Violence. Retrieved from https://www.blackburncenter.org/post/2020/02/26/black-women-domestic-violence

Ethnicity and Health in America Series: Substance Abuse and Addiction in the African-American Community. (n.d.). Retrieved from https://www.apa.org/pi/oema/resources/ethnicity-health/african-american/substance-abuse

Hamm, N. (2016, May 17). African-American Women and Depression. Retrieved from https://psychcentral.com/lib/african-american-women-and-depression#1